CAVALRY OF THE WEHRMACHT

Klaus Christian Richter

Kettledrummer of the 18th Cavalry Regiment (1938). His horse wears standard equipment with saddle blanket in accordance with the decree of November 2, 1937, which also laid down the shape and emblems of the draperies and tassels which adorned the kettledrum.

CAVALRY OF THE WEHRMACHT

1941-1945

Klaus Christian Richter

Schiffer Military History
Atglen, PA

Translated from the German by David Johnston.

Printed in the United States of America.
ISBN: 0-88740-814-1

This book was originally published under the title,
Kavallerie der Wehrmacht,
by Podzun-Pallas Verlag.

We are interested in hearing from authors with book ideas on related topics.

Published by Schiffer Publishing Ltd.
77 Lower Valley Road
Atglen, PA 19310
Please write for a free catalog.
This book may be purchased from the publisher.
Please include $2.95 postage.
Try your bookstore first.

CONTENTS

The greatcoat for non-commissioned officers and enlisted men was made of field-grey, in some cases quite coarse, cloth; as a result it was jokingly referred to as the "horse blanket." This was the sole protection against the cold for soldiers of the Reichsheer and later the Wehrmacht until 1942. After a maneuver two cavalry buglers give the signal to "assemble." Easily discernable is the so-called "martingale," whose purpose was to prevent the saddle from slipping. It was dropped

INTRODUCTION

Klaus Christian Richter has followed his two previous books on the history of the German cavalry with a third volume which deals with the complex organization, armament, equipment and training of the cavalry from the formation of the Reichswehr in 1919 to the last four fully-mounted horse regiments of the Ist (Army) Cavalry Corps, which were disbanded in Württemberg by the US Army in June 1945.

Employing his typical thoroughness and clear descriptive style, the author has succeeded in creating a clear picture of the former cavalry, enhanced by many original photos, drawings, etc. This is all the more admirable, since as a member of the 1935 age class he did not personally experience the events described herein, but instead had to assemble the necessary material through extensive research.

Following a look back at the eighteen horse regiments of the Reichswehr, the book describes their further development into cavalry regiments with the expansion of the Wehrmacht in 1935, then their disbandment with the formation of divisional reconnaissance battalions at the start of the Second World War in 1939, and finally the rebirth of the German army cavalry in 1943 with at first three cavalry regiments, and finally their ultimate disbandment by the US Army in June 1945.

It is clear even from this brief description what an enormous degree of operational readiness was required of the field forces in order to carry out such an extensive formation of new, capable formations and units within the shortest possible time. This is particularly relevant to the war years 1943-1945, during which other branches of the service received scarcely any personnel or material replacements.

In addition to providing precise descriptions of the weapons and equipment used, which were among the most modern of their day, the author reveals the German cavalry's very high standard of training, especially among the officers and NCOs. Beginning in peacetime, the cavalry gave priority to the training of man and horse. This state of affairs continued, even in the war years 1943-1945. Training was carried out between actions during brief rest periods, behind the main line of resistance, sometimes even in the positions when the combat situation allowed. This training shaped the horsemen, gave them confidence, allowed them to perform tremendous feats in the true spirit of the cavalry in spite of the severest psychological and physical burdens. This was also true of the difficult battles of withdrawal in the second half of the war right up to the end, when the collapse of the war and home fronts was imminent. The old soldierly virtues proved themselves once more: courage, sense of duty, feeling of responsibility, loyalty, comradeship, and as well love of the horse. Only thus was it possible for the troops to hold together until the last day and in June 1945 ride battalion after battalion into the cities of Württemberg.

The year 1945 marked the end of a tradition-rich, proud branch of the service which over the centuries had been able to pin great success to its banners. When the German Bundeswehr was formed in 1955 the cavalry was sacrificed to modern technology and motorization.

The cavalry spirit nevertheless lives on in the present-day armored reconnaissance battalions and in the units of the airborne brigades, which have assumed the role of the former cavalry and in part also its traditions.

The cavalry arm depicted in this book will undoubtedly awaken old memories in former cavalrymen, and perhaps it will also serve in many respects as an example today and tomorrow to the soldiers of the Bundeswehr and those of the younger generation who are involved in equestrian sports.

Stuttgart, autumn 1994

Conrad Müller
Rittmeister, retired
last commander of the 9th (Heavy) Troop, 32nd Horse Regiment

A horse troop of the 13th Cavalry Regiment prior to the parade held in honor of Hitler's fiftieth birthday on April 20, 1939.

HISTORICAL DEVELOPMENT

With passage of the Law for the Building-up of the Armed Forces on March 16, 1935, the former Reichswehr was transformed into the Wehrmacht. The Reichswehr, which had been imposed upon the German Reich by the Treaty of Versailles following the First World War, consisted of 100,000 men, and it was the will of the victors that it should not be an army in the actual sense. This was made quite clear in Article 160 of the treaty: "The army is intended solely for the maintenance of order within the German Empire and for the policing of its borders." In order to ensure that this provision remained unchanged in the long run, the terms of the treaty placed binding limits on the numerical size of the German Armed Forces and dictated its material equipment to the last detail. The use of all modern weapons, for example heavy artillery, tanks and aircraft, but also anti-tank and anti-aircraft guns, was forbidden. Even the use of motor vehicles for military purposes was severely restricted, a fact that has often been forgotten even by military experts.

Not only did the Treaty of Versailles ban certain weapons, it also dictated the organization and structure of the German Army. According to the provisions of the treaty seven infantry divisions and three cavalry divisions were to be formed, commanded by two army group headquarters.

Autumn maneuvers by the IXth Army Corps in Bavaria 1935. A cavalry troop assembles on a village street. The photo gives an impression of the arms and equipment used by the cavalry in the early years of the Wehrmacht. Note the typical steel helmets with ear cutouts, which the service referred to as the "cavalry helmet." The standard weapon was the Karabiner 98b carbine. Sergeants and machine-gunners were armed with the Pistole 08 sidearm.

The riders' mounts were outstanding specimens, trained during the Reichswehr period; they are wearing Packtaschen 34 saddlebags and rear saddle pack.

All told, the ten divisions consisted of the following units:

"- 21 infantry regiments
"- 18 cavalry regiments
"- 7 artillery regiments
"- 7 pioneer battalions
"- 7 signals battalions
"- 7 motor transport battalions
"- 7 supply train battalions
"- 7 medical battalions

With a total of eighteen regiments, the cavalry was heavily represented in the new army. The major role played by the cavalry is even more apparent when one looks at the numbers; of the 100,000 men of the Reichsheer, 16,400 were horsemen.

The former Entente allocated such a large cavalry force to the German Reich because it believed that it was safe to assume that an out-of-date cavalry equipped with lances would pose no great threat. One other consideration was the "- for that time "-relatively high cost of procuring and maintaining the cavalry's horses. These financial resources could not be used by Germany for other military purposes.

An Inter-allied Military Control Commission monitored Germany's military to ensure that all of the treaty's bans, provisions and conditions were maintained. It was authorized to inspect units of the Reichswehr at any time, even without warning, to uncover possible violations or even just to voice complaints.

Under these circumstances there was nothing that the Chief of the Army Command, a post held by Generaloberst von Seeckt from 1920 to 1926, could do but make the best of the situation.

Until about 1928 the horse regiments (Reiter-Regimenter) of the Reichswehr were organized as follows:

Regimental headquarters with bugle corps
1 signals platoon
4 (field) troops, each of 4 officers, 170 men and 200 horses
1 replacement and training troop of 4 officers, 110 men and 170 horses
1 heavy machine-gun platoon equipped with four s.MG. 08 (water-cooled)

A provision of the Inter-allied Military Control Commission required the heavy machine-gun platoon to be divided into two half-platoons based at two separate locations.

Seven of the horse regiments had an additional troop; in action each was to be placed under the command of an infantry division for reconnaissance duties. Each divisional troop had a strength of 4 officers, 150 men and 180 horses.

The Reichswehr cavalry had at its disposal a total of 97 troops.

At first the horseman was armed with the Karabiner 98a rifle with bayonet, the enlisted man's saber, and the 3.2-meter steel-tube lance. Later each horse platoon was assigned a "light" MG 08/15 water-cooled machine-gun.

The Allies intentionally specified this World War One standard of organization and equipment, in order to leave the Reichsheer in a state of inferiority compared to other European armies.

Not until the Inter-Allied Military Control Commission ceased its activities in 1926 was the Reichswehr able to begin cautiously reorganizing the cavalry. The lances were "retired" on

The Reichsheer cavalry was armed with the 3.2-meter-long steel-tube lance until 1927. This traditional weapon undoubtedly gave the horse troops a picturesque appearance, but it impeded the cavalry's development into a fast, firearm-equipped force.

The Training Troop of the 1st (Prussian) Horse Regiment, seen here in Insterburg, East Prussia on October 26, 1925 on the occasion of the dedication of the memorial to the 9th Light Infantry Horse Regiment of the old Imperial Army.

Below: This postcard from the Wahn Troop Training Grounds, now Cologne-Bonn airport, from the year 1938 depicts the weapons used by a cavalry regiment, with the exception of the armored scout car: the horseman with enlisted man's saber and Kar 98b carbine, the 37-mm anti-tank gun, the Gewehr 98 rifle carried by soldiers on foot, the Light Infantry Gun 18 (Cavalry Gun), and the sMG 08 water-cooled heavy machine-gun.

11

October 3, 1927. The Karabiner 98a, whose performance was somewhat limited, was replaced by the Karabiner 98b, whose dimensions and ballistics were fully comparable to those of the Gewehr 98.

The cavalry was now able to fight dismounted in the same way as the infantry. The object was to turn the cavalry into a "fast firearm-equipped force." In order to achieve this, however, further supporting weapons were required which were still forbidden by the Treaty of Versailles. One interim measure was the use of so-called "wooden guns" to represent cavalry guns and later anti-tank cannon in training and field exercises. In this way it was hoped that foreign objections could be avoided in the beginning.

After Germany left the League of Nations in 1933, the wooden mock-ups were replaced by real guns, which at first were designated "mine projectors" in order to conceal their true purpose. In 1933 the phoney anti-tank guns of the horse regiments gave way to true anti-tank platoons, although they were still horse-drawn. The first significant changes in the cavalry took place in autumn 1934. The 11th, 12th and 16th Horse Regiments were reequipped as motorized rifle regiments or motorcycle battalions. Many other horse regiments were forced to release entire troops for the formation of tank, anti-tank and armored reconnaissance units. Then in 1935 the 4th and 7th Horse Regiments were reorganized as panzer regiments.

Reiter-Rgt.	1. 4. 34	1. 10. 34	15. 10. 35	6. 10. 36	12. 10. 37	10. 11. 38
1.	Tilsit Insterburg 1. KB/1. KD	Insterburg 5. RB/Kav.K	Insterburg 5. RB/I	Reit. Insterburg 1. KB/I	Insterburg 1. KB/I	Insterburg 1. KB/I
2.	Osterode Allenstein 1. KB/1. KD	Angerburg 5. RB/Kav.K	Angerburg 5. RB/I	Reit. Angerburg 1. KB/I	Angerburg 1. KB/I	Angerburg 1. KB/I
3.	Rathenow Stendal 1. KD	Rathenow Stendal 4. RB/2. KD	Rathenow Stendal 4. RB/2. KD	Kav. vl. Rathenow vl. Stendal IX	I Göttingen II Göttingen IX	I Göttingen II Göttingen IX
4.	Potsdam Perleberg 1. KD	Potsdam = PzRgt. 6 1. RB/1. KD	Allenstein Osterode 5. RB/I	Reit. Allenstein Osterode 1. KB/I	Kav. I Allenstein II Allenstein 1. KB/I	I Allenstein II Allenstein 1. KB/I für I
5.	Stolp Belgard 2. KB/1. KD	Stolp 1. RB/1. KD	Stolp 1. RB/1. KD	Kav. Stolp II	I Stolp II Stolp II	I Stolp II Stolp II
6.	Pasewalk Schwedt Demmin 2. KB/1. KD	Schwedt 1. RB/1. KD	Schwedt 1. RB/1. KD	Kav. vl. Schwedt III	I Darmstadt II vl. Bensheim XII	I Darmstadt II vl. Bensheim s Darmstadt XII
7.	Breslau Lüben KK Breslau/2. KD	Breslau = PzRgt. 2 3. RB/2. KD	— — —	— — —	— — —	— — —
8.	Brieg Oels Namslau KK. Breslau/2. KD	Brieg 3. RB/2. KD	Brieg Namslau 2. KD	Kav. Brieg Namslau VIII	I vl. Brieg II Oels VIII	I Oels II Oels VIII
9.	Fürstenwalde Beeskow KK Dresden/2. KD	Fürstenwalde Beeskow 4. RB/2. KD	Fürstenwalde Beeskow 4. RB/2. KD	Kav. Fürstenwalde vl. Beeskow III	I Fürstenwalde II Fürstenwalde III	I Fürstenwalde II Fürstenwalde III
10.	Züllichau Torgau KK Dresden/2. KD	Torgau 4. RB/2. KD	Torgau 2. KD	Kav. Torgau IV	I Torgau II Torgau IV	I Torgau II Torgau IV
11.	Neustadt/OS Ohlau Leobschütz } = Reit.Rgt.11 KK Breslau/2. KD (mot.)	— — —	— — —	— — —	— — —	I Stockerau** II Stockerau** XVII
12.	Dresden Grimma Großenhain } = Reit.Rgt.12 KK Dresden/2. KD (mot.)	— — —	— — —	— — —	— — —	— — —

Reiter-Rgt.	1. 4. 34	1. 10. 34	15. 10. 35	6. 10. 36	12. 10. 37	10. 11. 38
13.	*Hannover* Lüneburg 3. KB/3. KD	*Hannover* Lüneburg 2. RB/1. KD	*Hannover* Lüneburg 2. RB/1. KD	*Kav. Lüneburg* X	I *Lüneburg* II Lüneburg X	I *Lüneburg* II Lüneburg X
14.	*Ludwigslust* Parchim Schleswig 3. KB/3. KD	*Ludwigslust* Parchim 2. RB/1. KD	*Ludwigslust* Parchim 2. RB/1. KD	*Kav. Ludwigslust* Parchim XI	I *Parchim* II *Ludwigslust* XI	I Parchim II *Ludwigslust* XI
15.	*Paderborn* Neuhaus Münster 3. KD	*Paderborn* Neuhaus 2. RB/1. KD?	*Paderborn* Neuhaus VI	*Kav. Paderborn* Neuhaus VI	I Neuhaus II *Paderborn* VI	I Neuhaus II *Paderborn* VI
16.	*Erfurt* Hofgeismar Langensalza 3. KD	} = Reit.Rgt.16 (mot.)	— ... —	— .— —	— — —	— — —
17.	*Bamberg* Ansbach Straubing 3. KD	*Bamberg* 6. RB/Kav.K	*Bamberg* VII	*Kav. Bamberg* VII	I *Bamberg* II Bamberg XIII	I *Bamberg* II Bamberg XIII
18.	*Stuttg.-Cannstatt* Ludwigsburg 3. KD	*Cannstatt* 6. RB/Kav.K	*Cannstatt* V	*Kav. Stuttg.-Cannstatt* Münsingen V	I vl. *Stuttgart* II Stuttgart V	I vl. *Stuttgart* sp. *Bruchsal* II Bruchsal V

Reiter-Rgt.   *Horse Regiment*   *Bicycle Battalion*
Radfahrer Bataillon

Abbreviations:
Kav.K = Cavalry Corps   KD = Cavalry Division
KB = Cavalry Brigade   RB = Horse Brigade
KK = Cavalry Detachment   Reit.Rgt. = Horse Regiment
     ** = taken on strength from the Austrian Federal Army on 1/4/1938

Signals wagon with six-horse team belonging to a horse regiment.

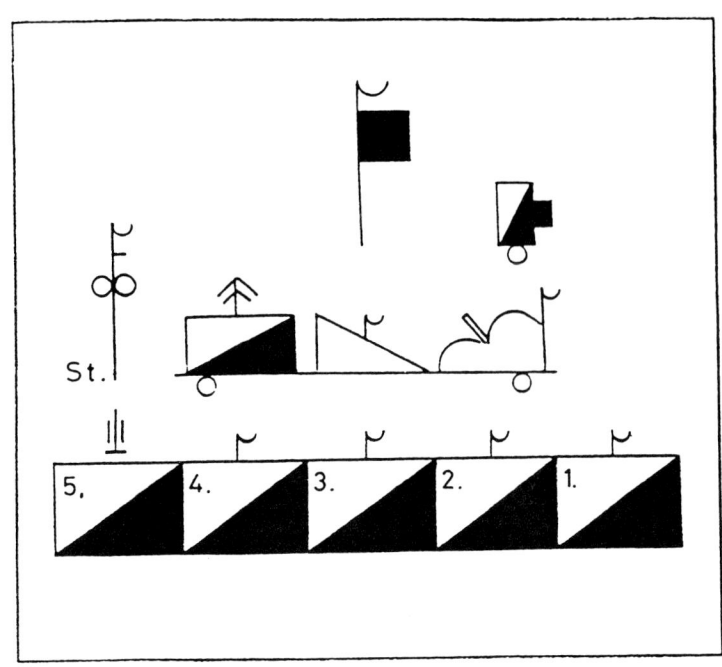

The organization of a horse regiment (above) and a cavalry regiment (below).

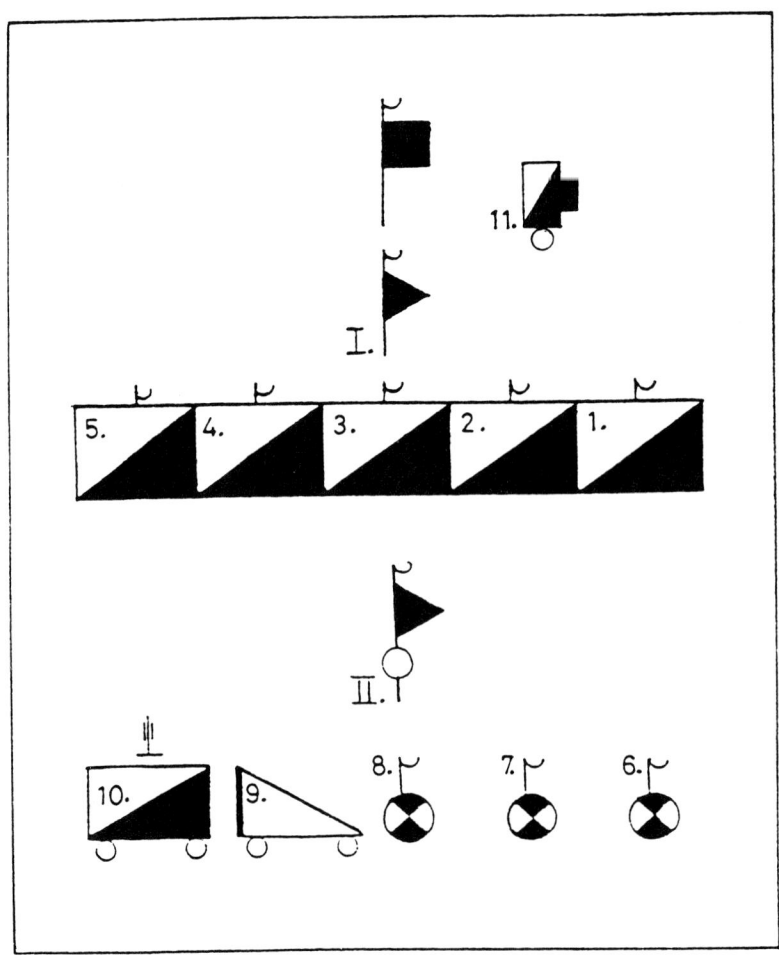

THE REBUILDING OF THE ARMY 1935-1938

In its initial form, the new German Wehrmacht (Armed Forces) created in 1935 had thirteen horse regiments. These quickly grew back to full strength; on the one hand because of the return, also in 1935, of universal compulsory military service (forbidden to Germany after the First World War), and on the other as a result of the incorporation of the mounted formations of the State Police as well as the enlistment of former officers of the old army and the Reichswehr.

The modernization and expansion of the cavalry began in 1936. The first examples of the Karabiner 98k rifle, which was to replace the Karabiner 98b and Gewehr 98, had been delivered to the army in the winter of 1934-35. The MG 34 was gradually replacing the l.MG 13 (Dreyse) "- which had been introduced into service with the cavalry "- and the s.MG. 08 (water-cooled) machine-guns. The horse-drawn anti-tank platoons became motorized units equipped with 37-mm anti-tank guns.

Transformation of the former horse (Reiter) regiments into cavalry (Kavallerie) regiments was initiated with the formation of an armored scout platoon, a motorized pioneer platoon and a bicycle troop by each regiment. In East Prussia the 1st and 2nd Horse Regiments received no bicycle troops and an armored scout squad with three vehicles instead of an armored scout platoon. As the bulk of their personnel remained horse-mounted, they retained the designation "Reiter-Regiment."

By 1938 the bicycle squadron developed into the partly-motorized IInd (Bicycle) Battalion, as a result of which each cavalry regiment grew to eleven troops.

The 4th Horse Regiment, which had been reorganized as a panzer regiment in 1935, was reestablished as a cavalry regiment in 1936 at Allenstein, East Prussia. This was followed in 1938 by the restoration of the 11th Cavalry Regiment, which was formed from the six troops of the Austrian Federal Army at Stockau, near Vienna.

Drawing illustrating how the light machine-gun was carried by a cavalry section.

The thirteen cavalry regiments were designated corps units and each was placed under the direct command of a non-motorized army corps. Its task was to provide each infantry or alpine division of the corps with a partly-motorized reconnaissance battalion. These regiments thus filled the role of the traditional troop cavalry (Truppenkavellerie).

On the other hand, the 1st and 2nd Horse Regiments, together with the 1st Bicycle Battalion, the 1st Horse Artillery Battalion and other units, formed the 1st Cavalry Brigade at Insterburg, East Prussia. This brigade was thus the sole Army Cavalry Unit of the German Armed Forces.

Organization and Strengths of a Horse Regiment

Unit	Officers	NCOs	Corporals	Enlisted Men	Horses	Horses Total
31st Horse Regiment						
HQ 1st Horse Rgt.	12+2 *(includes 3 veterinary officers and 5 officials)*	18+1	18	12	28 R, 4 Re	33
HQ Troop, 1st Horse Rgt.	2	14+1	4	11	–	–
Signals Platoon, 1st Horse Rgt.	1	9	11	27	20 R, 3 Re, 4 Z	27
1st Troop, 1st Horse Rgt.	5	41+1	45	106	176 R, 17 Re	193
2nd Troop, 1st Horse Regiment	5	41+1	45	106	176 R, 17 Re	193
3rd Troop, 1st Horse Rgt.	5	41 + 1	45	106	176 R, 17 Re	193
4th Troop, 1st Horse Rgt.	5	41+1	45	106	176 R, 17 Re	193
5th Troop, 1st Horse Rgt.	5	41+1	43	99	140 R, 14 Re	154
Bugler Corps, 1st Horse Regiment	1	21	3	3	29 R, 3 Re	32
Total:	41+2	267+7	259	576	922 R, 92 re, 4 Z	1,018
					1,152 soldiers	1,018 horses

Re. Columns 2 and 3: + 2 = 2 medical officers or 1 medical NCO
Re. Column 6: R = saddle horse, Re = remount, Z = draft horse

For comparison: Authorized strength after mobilization	Officers	NCOs	Corporals and enlisted men	Horses
	41	204		1,195
		1,440 soldiers		1,421

THE INFANTRY HORSE PLATOONS

Two further cavalry-related innovations were introduced as part of the reformation of the army: the infantry horse platoons and the military area remount schools. As of 1935 each active infantry regiment was supposed to receive an infantry horse platoon for the reconnaissance and security roles. Each platoon had a strength of 32 men and 33 horses. Although units of the State Police were draw upon for the formation of these new units, the bulk of the officers and NCOs, and even entire platoons, came from the cavalry.

In general, training and employment of these platoons followed the principles contained in current cavalry service manuals. The Inspector of Cavalry was responsible for their supervision.

THE MILITARY AREA RIDING AND DRIVING SCHOOLS

The Reichswehr had a cavalry school which was retained by the Wehrmacht. Located in Hanover, it served primarily to train replacement officers and riding and driving instructors. It also cultivated all aspects of the sport of riding.

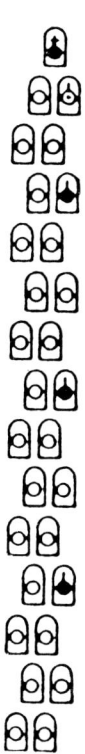

Infantry horse platoon in march order (without combat train). Combat train: 1 Hf 1 with two-horse team, 2 men, 1 bicyclist.

So-called Military Area Remount Schools were set up in order to relieve the infantry, but also other branches of the armed forces which had mounted or horse-drawn units, of the responsibility of training saddle and draft horses. The first school of this type was created in 1933 in Soltau (Military Area X). By 1938 all thirteen military areas had such training establishments. In 1937 the schools were redesignated "Military Area Riding and Driving Schools," as their area of responsibility had been expanded in scope to include riding and driving courses for officers, reserve officers and non-commissioned officers. The cavalry provided the majority of the expert personnel for this new training organization and many former officers of the old army returned to serve there. During the war women made up a considerable part of the non-commissioned officer corps of the schools, releasing the men for front-line service.

As a result of establishing these schools, which remained in existence until 1945, the infantry, signals units, pioneers, medical units and to some extent the supply units, received a large percentage of their saddle and draft horses fully-trained. Only the cavalry and the artillery trained their own remounts in the replacement battalions.

The 1st EAST PRUSSIAN CAVALRY BRIGADE, LATER 1st CAVALRY DIVISION

In peacetime the bulk of the German cavalry was organized into thirteen cavalry regiments, which on mobilization had to dispatch selected reconnaissance battalions (troop cavalry) to the infantry divisions.

In East Prussia, however, the army had a cavalry brigade whose role was that of an experimental unit; it was to determine whether mounted army cavalry still had a role in a modern war.

The peacetime organization of the brigade included the following units:

1st Horse Regiment, Insterburg
2nd Horse Regiment, Angerburg
1st Bicycle Battalion, Tilsit
1st Horse Artillery Battalion, Insterburg
4th Cavalry Regiment, Allenstein and Osterode
1st Motorized Reconnaissance Battalion, Königsberg

All of the cavalry units in Military Area I had been combined into a brigade, mainly for organizational reasons, but also to ensure a uniform standard of training.

Unlike the other cavalry units, however, with mobilization the 1st Cavalry Brigade was supposed to assume a wartime organization that differed significantly from that of peacetime:

Brigade Headquarters
>   with dispatch rider platoon

1st Horse Regiment
>   with motorized signals platoon
>   4 horse troops
>>   (each with 9 light and 4 heavy machine-guns)
>   1 heavy troop
>>   (4 cavalry guns, 6 heavy mortars)
>   1 headquarters troop with
>>   armored scout platoon (3 armored scout cars)
>>   anti-tank platoon (3 ant-tank guns 37-mm)
>>   pioneer platoon (3 light machine-guns)

2nd Horse Regiment (same organization as 1st Regiment)

Bicycle Battalion with
>   motorized signals platoon
>   3 bicycle troops
>   (each with 9 light machine-guns, 4 heavy machine-guns, 3 light mortars)
>   1 heavy troop with
>>   1 anti-tank platoon (3 anti-tank guns 37-mm)
>>   2 cavalry gun platoons (each with 2 cavalry guns)
>>   1 mortar platoon (6 heavy mortars)

Horse Artillery Battalion with
>   headquarters battery
>   3 horse batteries (each with 4 cannon 75-mm)

Anti-Tank Company (motorized, prime mover) with
>   12 anti-tank guns 37-mm

Machine-Gun Company (motorized, prime mover) with
>   12 anti-aircraft guns 20-mm

Pioneer Company

Signals Company

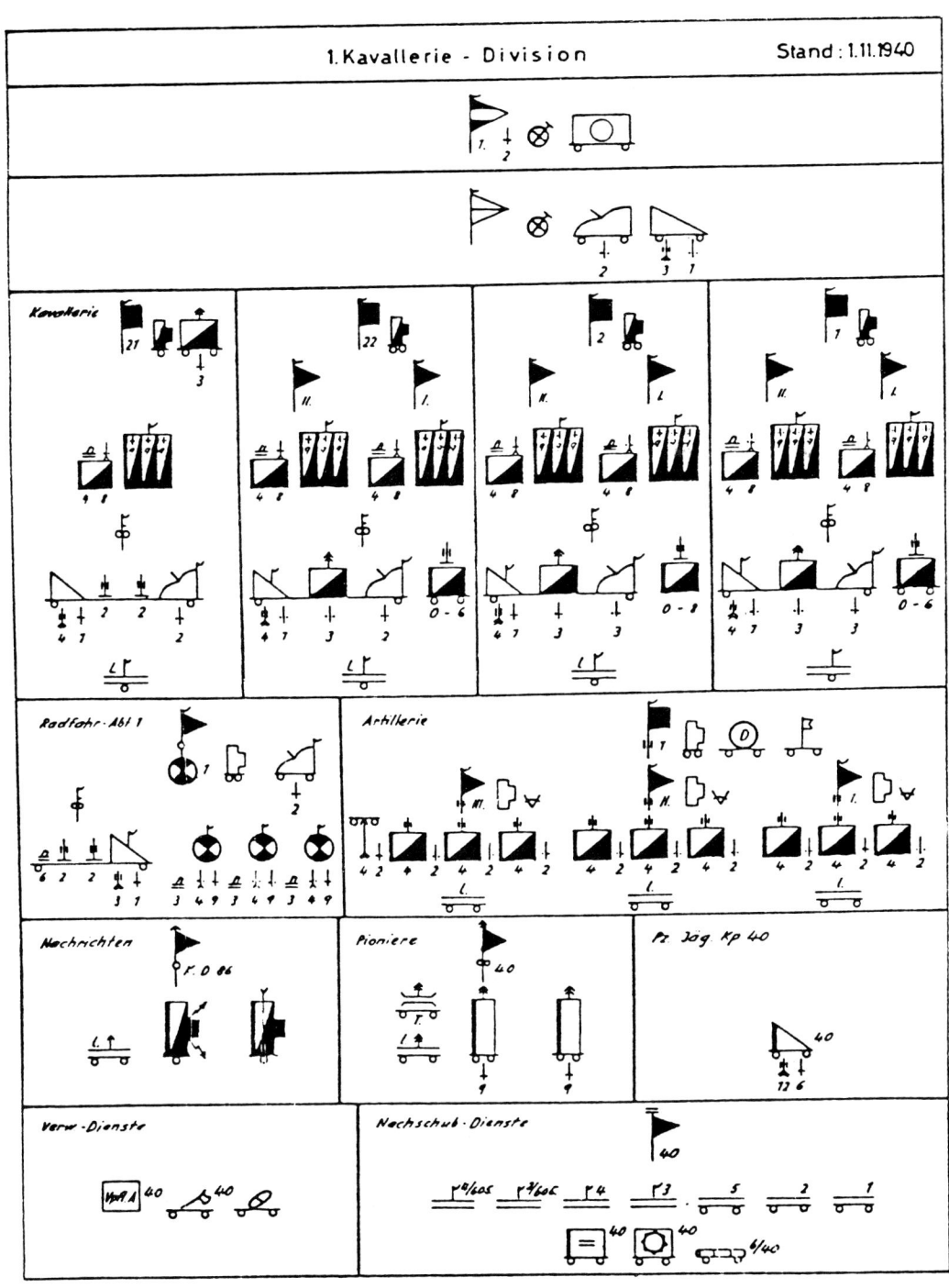

Order of battle of the 1st Cavalry Division on November 1, 1940.

19

Supply Service with
    HQ Brigade Supply Officer
    2 light motor vehicle transport columns (30 t)
    2 horse-drawn transport columns
    1 light motor vehicle transport column for fuel
    1 workshop platoon
    1 supply platoon
Administration Service with
    medical company (motorized)
    ambulance platoon
    veterinary company

Organized in this way the cavalry brigade achieved a strength of:

6,684 men
4,552 horses
409 horse-drawn vehicles
427 cars and trucks
318 motorcycles (153 with sidecars)
6 armored scout cars

With its modern heavy weapons and long-distance communications the brigade was a capable large-size unit with a high degree of mobility in all types of terrain; however when the Polish Campaign began in 1939 the planned organization had not been achieved.

The planned anti-tank company, the machine-gun company (20-mm) and the signals company had not been sent at all, while the horse artillery battalion had only two active batteries and the supply services had been reduced in size.

In spite of this considerable reduction in fighting strength the brigade proved a success during the war in Poland, which led to the formation of the 1st Cavalry Division on October 25, 1939. In the process, however, eleven reconnaissance battalions were forced to give up their horse troops.

The cavalry division fought in Holland, Belgium and France during the campaign in Western Europe in 1940.

In late summer 1940 the division was transferred to Poland into the so-called Generalgouvernement, where it remained until the start of the campaign against Russia in 1941.

For the attack in the east the Cavalry Division was placed under the command of Panzergruppe 2 (Guderian). True the division was able to match the offensive tempo of the armored units; however at times during this operation it proved impossible to adequately supply the 17,000 cavalry horses. Inevitably the unit's fighting strength suffered. At its own request the division was reequipped as the 24th Panzer Division during the winter of 1941-42. For the time being the army cavalry had ceased to exist.

In the year 1942 the army had at its disposal exclusively troop cavalry in the form of division reconnaissance battalions, many of which no longer had horse troops.

The 17,000 horses of the former 1st Cavalry Division, which had been carefully trained for a specific purpose during the long years of peace at great cost in time and money, were turned over to the collection detachments of infantry divisions and to eastern mounted troops, which to a large degree amounted to a waste of a valuable asset.

UNIFORMS AND EQUIPMENT

The army of the Wehrmacht wore a standard uniform in field gray similar to that used by the Reichsheer from 1920 to 1934. The only exception was the armored command, created in 1934-35, which wore a field uniform whose basic color was black.

The standard field-grey uniform worn by the cavalry and the horse-mounted elements of other branches of the service differed significantly from that of the infantry, however. While prior to the introduction of the Stahlhelm 35 the Stalhelm 18 had been the standard helmet used by the army, the cavalry wore the "steel helmet with ear cutouts," which subsequently came to be known as the "cavalry helmet." All riders wore riding boots instead of hobnailed marching boots (Knobelbecher, or jackboots). The leg of the riding boot was eight to twelve centimeters longer; it was also made of softer, thinner leather in order to better fit the saddle. Besides the toe of the boot had to fit easily into the stirrup. In contrast to the marching boot, the soles of the riding boot were generally not hobnailed. Following the completion of rider training all horse-mounted personnel wore buckled spurs. The riding boots were worn with breeches made of stone-grey fabric with leather trimmings. Made of calfskin, suede or goatskin, the leather trimmings covered the bottom half of the seat, the crotch and the inner sides of the legs to below the knee. Due to shortages of the appropriate material, riding pants manufactured during the war often had trimmings of uniform fabric.

The rider had no field pack or knapsack. Dismounted he wore the so-called "trooper pack" (the right-hand Type 34 saddlebag) with his tent square placed around it or rolled-up coat and mess kit buckled to it. The back of the right Type 34 saddlebag was fitted with carrying straps so that it could be worn on the back like the assault pack later used by the infantry. A new type of saddlebag was introduced in 1940; in this case the trooper pack was worn on the back hooked into the belt carrier for cavalry.

In fact the tent square was the cavalryman's only protection from the rain, and his coat and woolen cap his only protection against the cold until the winter of 1941-42. Hence it follows, that the German army was unprepared for a winter campaign.

All horse-mounted soldiers wore the enlisted man's saber with their field and dress uniforms instead of a bayonet. On horseback the saber was stowed in a leather fixture on the right side of the saddle behind the rider; in the case of officers and sergeants the saber-holder was mounted on the left side of the saddle.

The service color of the Wehrmacht cavalry was gold, as it had been in the Reichswehr since 1920. This color was also worn by personnel of the cavalry schools and the thirteen military area riding and driving schools. Only the infantry horse platoons were assigned white as a service color and hence were also referred to as "white troopers."

A number of units, specifically the 1st and 2nd Troops of the 5th Cavalry Regiment, the 2nd and 4th Troops of the 6th Cavalry Regiment and the 4th Troop of the 13th Cavalry Regiment, wore metal badges on their headgear recalling former cavalry units. In the case of the 5th Cavalry Regiments it was the death's head of the two former Prussian lifeguard-hussar regiments, the 6th Cavalry Regiment the Swedte Eagle of the former Prussian Dragoons Regiment No. 2, and the 13th Cavalry Regiment the death's head of the former Hussar Regiment No. 17 of Brunswick. These memorial badges continued to be worn on garrison caps or were reintroduced during the war.

ARMAMENT AND EQUIPMENT

The authorized strength of a horse troop in peacetime was 5 officers, 42 non-commissioned officers and 151 enlisted men. In addition to the saber, which was carried by all horse-mounted soldiers, officers carried the Pistole 08 (or their own pistol) as a service weapon. After 1939 all non-commissioned officers in command positions were armed with the MP 38 submachine-gun and later the MP 40. All other NCOs and enlisted men, with the exception of machine-gunners, who were likewise armed with the Pistole 08, carried the Karabiner 98k carbine. Each of the nine horse squads had one MG 34 light machine-gun with anti-aircraft tripod (from 1940 only one tripod per platoon), while each troop included a machine-gun section with two MG 34 heavy machine-guns, later a machine-gun platoon with four MG 34 heavy machine-guns, as well as an ammunition section. The troop train consisted of a field kitchen, a large blacksmith wagon and an Hf 1 ammunition and weapons wagon; with mobilization these were joined by a series of other horse-drawn vehicles and a small number of trucks. As well in peacetime each troop had one motorcycle dispatch rider.

Prior to the start of the campaign against Russia the horse and bicycle troops were each issued two Panzerbüchse 39 anti-tank rifles.

The following items were part of the standard combat equipment of the troop:

> 20 pairs of binoculars
> 32 message blank pouches
> 20 prismatic compasses
> 125 shovels
> 23 pick mattocks
> 16 wire cutters
> 5 compass saws
> 10 claw axes
> 4 flare pistols
> 4 signal lamps
> 22 pairs of sunglasses
> 1 bugle

All equipment was carried the men or on the horses.

The peacetime strength of a bicycle troop, which was partially motorized, was 195 men. The three bicycle platoons were equipped with black-painted army bicycles; losses in the early campaigns were made good with bicycles purchased in Holland, Belgium and France. The troop headquarters detail, the machine-gun section, the mortar (50-mm) section, and the train achieved mobility through the use of motor vehicles capable of cross-country travel and motorcycles, some with sidecars.

The bicycle troop's equipment was largely similar to that of a horse troop, while its uniform was closer to that of an infantry company.

Bicycle riders were issued one additional item of clothing, a "cape for bicycle riders," which was rarely worn by horse-mounted soldiers. Motorcyclists wore the Kradmantel (motorcyclist coat), which enjoyed much popularity among the troops.

In addition to the nine light and two heavy machine-guns with which the horse troops were equipped, the bicycle troop had three 50-mm mortars, whose purpose was to supporting the platoons with high-angle fire during firefights.

When employed as part of a reconnaissance battalion, the bicycle troop in fact represented the unit's infantry firepower, possessing as it did its own high-angle weapons, while not having to detach a number of riflemen to tend the horses, as was inevitably the case with a horse troop.

The uniforms and equipment of motorized cavalry units was the same as other branches of the army equipped with motor vehicles. With the exception of the armored scout car sections, which by the way did not wear black special clothing, the role of the motorized troops was to transport heavy weapons, primarily the anti-tank guns (37mm) and the Light Infantry Gun 18 (l.IG. 18). With a caliber of 75mm, the l.IG. 18 was capable of high-angle or flat trajectory fire and was also called the "cavalry gun" by the horse-mounted soldiers.

THE TRAINING OF THE CAVALRY

In the Reichswehr, as in the old army, rider training was the focal point of daily duty. Since enlisted men and NCOs served twelve years, it was possible to dedicate an extraordinary amount of time to rider training. 3,000 hours of riding was the specified norm for training a simple trooper.

This changed abruptly in 1935, when Germany regained military sovereignty and compulsory military service was introduced. In the beginning compulsory service lasted one year. As the cavalry was permitted to enlist a maximum of only 10% volunteers, the majority of the men to be trained were draftees with only twelve months in which to learn to ride.

Ride training was reduced to one hour per day on average. The focus now was on training in weapons and firing as well as combat tactics. In spite of its specialized reconnaissance and scouting roles, the cavalry was required to carry out the same amount of weapons and firing training as the infantry.

The essence of cavalry warfare consisted of the transition from fast, at that time wide-ranging, movements in any weather and any terrain to fighting dismounted according to the operational tenets of the infantry. Consequently the cavalry had to practice marches on horseback in addition to actual combat tactics. Distances of 50 to 100 kilometers per day, even for several days, were considered the norm, and it should be borne in mind that the weakest rider set the pace for the entire unit and that the horses had to carry a weight (rider, equipment and weapons) of 2 to 2.5 hundredweight.

Such feats could only be achieved through systematic training. That they were possible at all is largely due to the high-quality, carefully-trained horse material and the availability of large numbers of riding instructors. The foundations for both of these factors were laid in the quiet work done by the Reichswehr in the fifteen years of peace between 1919 and 1934.

One other important point in the training of the cavalry was the crossing of bodies of water with, but especially without, the support of combat engineers. In peacetime each horse and cavalry regiment was required to conduct at least one large-scale crossing exercise per year.

As army cavalry, the horse regiments had their own motorized pioneer platoons in their headquarters troops. These included in their equipment large and small pneumatic floats, later designated as inflatable boats.

Cavalry regiments, on the other hand, possessed no organic pioneer units. The horse troops of the divisional reconnaissance battalions therefore usually had to ford or swim bodies of water. The equipment sections of the battalions had two large and two small pneumatic floats for use by the bicycle and heavy troops. Beyond that the reconnaissance battalion was dependent on its division's pioneer battalion.

In the cavalry special emphasis was placed on the development of speed of thought and action. A typical example of this is the "field order," which as a concept was passed on to and used by the armored forces after there were no more troopers.

The training provided a bicycle squadron was largely similar to that of an infantry company. Bicycle riding in itself did not have to be taught, and the correct tactical use of bicycles within the framework of a unit or part of a unit required nowhere near the same amount of time that comparable training in a horse troop did. However, as bicycle troops could also be called upon to carry out reconnaissance duties, further training was required in that area.

Given favorable road conditions, a bicycle patrol could cover greater distances more quickly than horsemen and make virtually no noise while doing so. Where there was a well-developed system of main and secondary roads bicycle patrols frequently took less time than mounted patrols to cover the same distance.

The divisional reconnaissance battalions formed later in the war received an additional bicycle troop in place of the horse troop. Ultimately some divisions had to make do with a single reinforced bicycle troop as their reconnaissance organ. The sole reason for this was that there were no more trained riders available. Taken altogether, the bicycle troops were an unqualified success in the campaign in Western Europe. In Eastern and Southeastern Europe terrain and road conditions put them to a severe test, especially after the onset of the muddy period, which ultimately deprived the bicycle troops of their mobility.

In the heavy troops the operational routine and thus the focal points of training were determined by technology. The mobile style of warfare waged by cavalry and bicycle troops required the heavy weapons to adapt their fighting style to theirs in order to ensure a close cooperation. This process was made somewhat easier due to the fact that many officers and NCOs had been forced to transfer from the cavalry to the heavy troops, especially during the years of expansion.

The signals troops and platoons were somewhat unique, combining as they did horsemen, horse-drawn vehicles and motor vehicles, a mixture which did not exactly simplify organization and command. As would be expected, the training provided radio operators and telephonists was identical to that of the other branches of the service.

The missions assigned to the horse troops of reconnaissance battalions led to a requirement to train some radio operators to ride. The signals platoons of horse regiments were originally equipped with horse-drawn signals equipment trailers, which served to transport both radio and field telephone equipment. In the course of the partial motorization of the cavalry, especially the allocation of armored scout cars, a part of the signals equipment was also motorized. Neither signals equipment trailers nor motor vehicles were particularly well suited to the reconnaissance and patrol duties of the horse-mounted units. Consequently mounted radio and field telephone squads had to be formed, whose primary role was to accompany mounted patrols into action.

The 1st Cavalry Division, which as army cavalry had largely different roles to fill than the troop cavalry, retained the six-horse-drawn signals equipment wagon as standard equipment until its conversion to an armored unit.

How the cavalry saw itself is revealed in this interesting contemporary account from the year 1939:

THE VERSATILITY OF THE CAVALRY

by Leutnant Elert of the 17th Cavalry Regiment

The development of military technology has given the cavalry a new face. The masses of horsemen charging to the attack have disappeared from the modern battlefield. Equally great demands are made of the cavalry as a reconnaissance and fighting force. The cavalry has been given fast, mobile elements and heavy weapons to enable it to deal with any situation. Today the cavalry encompasses every type of military role like no other branch of the service. The horse troops have been joined by bicycle and motorized troops.

There are many who cannot make friends with the horse. Unlike the farmer's son, whose association begins in his youth, those from the city in particular are often unable to develop an understanding and love of the horse. The cavalry bicyclist has the same role, with certain limitations, as the horseman. The bicycle patrol works its way toward the enemy over roads and paths no matter how narrow. No sound betrays them. They are completely independent of fuel and fodder. The bicyclist can advance as long as his strength allows.

Reconnaissance missions are not always without complications, however. The enemy does everything he can to prevent his cards from being seen. If the strength of the patrol is insufficient, bicycle infantry is called in. "Dismount for combat!" orders the officer. The bicycles disappear into the ditches, the infantry advance toward the enemy under the covering fire of their own light and heavy machine-guns and overcome the resistance. A whistle blast, a signal from the officer, and the bicyclists set out after the retreating enemy to prevent him from settling down again. Sore feet and chafed shoulders are foreign to both the horseman and the bicyclist. And when the bicyclist returns to his quarters at night he puts his "donkey" into the shed and is done. He is not at the end of his strength like the infantry, nor does he need to provide food and water for his horse. When a recruit joins a bicycle troop he does not need to learn to ride a horse or drive a motor vehicle. He has been able to ride a bicycle since his school years. All his training is concentrated on becoming a soldier. He learns to handle weapons "- the rifle, the pistol, the light and heavy machine-gun and the mortar. He learns how to act in the field as well as the patrol and reconnaissance duties of the cavalryman.

In the IInd Battalion of a cavalry regiment, however, friends of the motor and the artillery will find everything they desire. The motorized troops are made up of armored scout, anti-tank and cavalry gun platoons. Heavily armored and equipped with powerful motors and weapons, the armored scout cars drive deep into enemy territory. Their mission is long-range reconnaissance: where is the enemy, where is he concentrating his main forces, what are his intentions? Reconnaissance in a armored scout car demands real men. Far more than the horseman or bicyclist, the man in the armored scout car must have a clear head and his heart in the right place. The enemy can appear beyond any bend in the road, in any wood. The armored scout car crewman's best protection is his own keen mind and his ability to make decisions, the speed of his vehicle and not last its armor. Should the enemy bar the way, then he needs his weapons and the speed provided by his motor. The armored car is gone before the enemy can fire. Should the patrol encounter an enemy barricade, then it fires smoke candles which blind the enemy and make it easier the armored cars to withdraw. The dispatch rider and the radio operator are the patrol leader's indispensable helpers. Those with an interest in communications can combine the thrill of armored patrol duty with the technology of the radio and become a radio operator in an armored car. The motorcycle sport rider can demonstrate his ability and intrepidity while serving as a dispatch rider. If for some reason the radio reports fail to get through, often the radio-equipped armored car is put out of action, then the dispatch rider must give his all.

The hunter can satisfy his passion in the anti-tank platoon. Out of sight, camouflaged in a ditch, concealed behind a bush or fence, the defensive specialist waits behind his gun. His patience and stamina are often put to a severe test. For hours nothing moves, until suddenly the enemy is there, as if sprouted from the earth. Weeks of training in aiming in fractions of a second, confidence in serving the gun, now prove their worth. The first shot must be on target, and if there are several enemy vehicles, each following shot must strike with the same precision. The anti-tank gunner's battle lasts only a few seconds. But in that short time the level of training and the teamwork of the crew are evident. Like the hunter after the fleeing wild animal, so is the anti-tank gunner after the speeding tank.

Finally there is the cavalry regiment's artillery. Should the machine-guns of the horse and bicycle troops be unable to dislodge the enemy, then the speedy vehicles move forward with the small artillery pieces. While the guns move into firing position behind cover just behind the front lines, the platoon headquarters squad, which has hurried up into the front lines, measures the range and bearing of the most dangerous targets. A brief firing command and the shells strike the target with razor-sharp precision. Through firing at short range and the precision work of the gun, the small cavalry guns have an effectiveness matched by few weapons. The hearts of the horsemen or bicyclists pinned down by the enemy fire are lifted: "There, that's brought relief!"

The cavalry encompasses all types of weapons activities like no other branch of the German Army. On the one hand, with its horse and bicycle troops and armored car platoons it is a reconnaissance and combat unit. On the other, horsemen and bicyclists are mobile infantry. Should the patrol encounter stiff enemy resistance, the cavalry possesses the offensive strength to break that resistance. Heavy machine-gun teams and cavalry gun platoons make things hot for the enemy and force him to give ground. The anti-tank platoon provides protection from enemy tanks. No enemy tank will succeed in seeing our hand when a cavalry anti-tank platoon is lying in wait.

The Horse Troop

As varied as the roles of a horse troop are, the motto always remains the same: "After the enemy!" The aggressive spirit of a Seydlitz, of a Zieten, lives on in our Wehrmacht's all-terrain force. Love and understanding of the horse, the horseman's most loyal comrade, is naturally a prerequisite, for only the horse is capable of going anywhere. Of course the time of massed cavalry charges is past, even though the missions have remained basically the same: reconnoiter and fight. Reconnaissance means tracking down the enemy, determining what the enemy is doing, and then staying on his heels. Courage and versatility must be demanded of every horseman, regardless of whether he is advancing through enemy territory alone on his horse, knowing that an important command decision perhaps rests on his report, or is far beyond his own lines as part of a patrol. But reconnaissance is not the only role of the cavalry, engaging the enemy in combat is also called for. Often the mission of a horse troop is to make contact with the enemy with the help of the horse, then attack and destroy him. The fighting style of a dismounted horse troop differs from that of the infantry in its greater versatility; frequently all or part of a mounted troop will disengage from the enemy, in order to ¨- by once again taking advantage of the horse ¨- attack him at another, more favorable place.

Again and again the horse steps to the forefront of cavalry duty.

So even during peacetime training we see schooling for the combat and reconnaissance roles going hand in hand with learning to ride and the proper care of the horse. Duties are especially multifaceted and thus varied in the summer half-year, when the individual horseman has the opportunity to put what he has learned during the winter to the test in large-scale exercises. No matter how large the scale of the exercise, the cavalry will always be given independent missions which demand a high degree of sense of duty and responsibility, of courage and versatility. In case of war a soldier inspired by the true cavalry spirit will be able to render invaluable service to his unit.

The first infantry horse platoons were formed in 1935. Apart from the white service color they scarcely differed from the platoons of the cavalry. In the photograph is the horse platoon of the 17th Infantry Regiment, Brunswick, following autumn maneuvers by the IXth Army Corps near Fritzlar in 1936.

THE TROOP CAVALRY IN THE SECOND HALF OF THE WAR

After the 1st Cavalry Division became the 24th Panzer Division in the winter of 1941-42, the only cavalry left in the German Army was in the form of the divisional reconnaissance battalions. With 85 battalions, however, this was still a considerable number. The reconnaissance battalions represented a significant asset to their divisions even long after the advance had given way to positional warfare or retreat.

Since their troops had to a large extent originated from active peacetime units, possessed a high degree of mobility, and had at their disposal a reasonable quota of heavy weapons, the reconnaissance battalions were often committed where the fighting was the fiercest. It was this that earned them the honorary title of "division fire-brigade." Of course the reconnaissance battalions were increasingly depleted in these actions and the time was near when this part of the cavalry, too, would have ceased to exist.

The creation of Cavalry Regiments Center, North and South saved the surviving horse troops as they were summoned for the formation of these new units.

The remnant reconnaissance battalions (without horse-mounted troops) were designated "Division Fusilier Battalions." They were brought up to strength and bolstered the infantry component of their divisions. In spite of the "Fusilier" title some retained their cavalry traditions and with it the gold service color. The 1st troop or company of each battalion retained its bicycles so as to be able to continue in the reconnaissance role. They remained in action in this form from 1943 until the end of the war.

For the sake of completeness it should be mentioned that some reconnaissance battalions, mostly in the west or in Italy, kept their previous designation and composition.

The reconnaissance assets of the lower levels of command, the infantry horse platoons, were reduced from three to two horse squads during the second half of the war. However, equipped with machine-guns and submachine-guns or assault rifles, they remained potent units and were employed by their regiments as a mobile reserve.

---

1 Battalion Headquarters, horse-mounted and motorized.

1st (Horse) Troop: personnel horse-mounted, organization and armament roughly comparable to that of the horse troop of a horse regiment.

2nd (Bicycle) Troop: personnel on bicycles, organization and armament roughly comparable to that of the bicycle troop of   a cavalry regiment.

3rd (Heavy) troop: motorized, consisting of:
*   1 armored car patrol*
*   1 cavalry gun platoon*
*   1 anti-tank platoon*

1 Signals Platoon: partly horse-mounted, partly motorized, with 1 radio section and 1 field-telephone section.

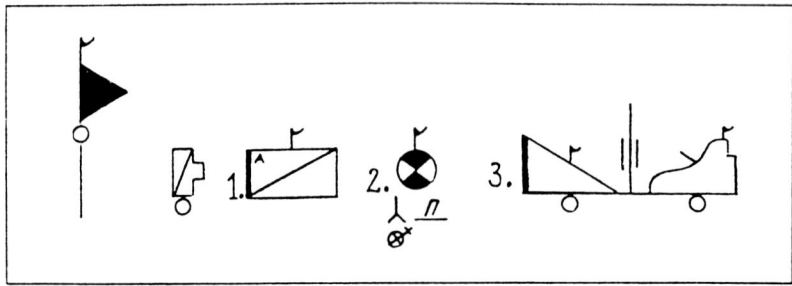

THE REBIRTH OF THE ARMY CAVALRY

Following several unsuccessful attempts to concentrate the remaining cavalry units in the east into effective units in 1942, at the beginning of 1943 then Rittmeister von Boeselager finally succeeded with the help of the Commander in Chief of Army Group Center, Generalfeldmarschall von Kluge.

The initial formation was dubbed "Cavalry Unit Boeselager." From it were formed three cavalry regiments which were placed under the command of Army Groups North, Center and South. Their success as mobile reserves was so impressive that they were reorganized into two cavalry brigades in 1944. The Ist Cavalry Corps was created just for them, to which the Hungarian Ist Cavalry Division was also subordinated. The still incomplete cavalry corps faced its first crucial test in June 1944, when Army Group Center collapsed within a few days. It contributed significantly to the stabilization of the resulting precarious situation. The corps subsequently saw action at the Narev and later in East Prussia. In December 1944 it was transferred to Hungary. There in March 1945 it participated in the last German offensive, code named "Awakening of Spring," which was supposed to regain the Danube Line. After the failure of the offensive the cavalry corps conducted a fighting withdrawal in the direction of Austria. After the surrender the still fully-intact unit was interned in Austria by British forces. Transported by rail to Württemberg and Hesse, in June 1945 the last German cavalry unit was disbanded by the Americans. The enlisted men were released after a short period in captivity and the officers followed soon afterward. The horses were turned over to local farmers for use in agriculture.

The Waffen-SS formed its own large cavalry units, initially a cavalry brigade in 1941, which was then enlarged into a division in 1942. In contrast to the former 1st Cavalry Division (of the Army), the SS Cavalry Division was well-equipped with anti-tank and anti-aircraft weapons. Following two years of unbroken service on the Eastern Front, at the beginning of 1944 the division gave up some of its elements to help form another SS cavalry division.

Both divisions were largely destroyed in the pocket surrounding Fortress Budapest, which fell on February 11, 1945.

In March a new SS cavalry Division was formed from the surviving remnants of the two divisions destroyed in Budapest together with Hungarian and Romanian volunteers. The new formation saw action, though not as a unit, north of Vienna until the German surrender.

Oberst von Pannwitz, who was formally named commander of all Cossack units serving in the German Army on November 8, 1942, pursued a plan to create a cavalry division from these loosely organized units. It was not until the actual Cossack lands had been lost that the formation of a Cossack Cavalry Division was ordered. The order took effect on April 21, 1943; the site chosen for the unit's formation was Mielau in East Prussia. After less than six months training the 1st Cossack Division was sent to Yugoslavia for use against Tito's partisans. Success avoided the division in the beginning, however its effectiveness and esprit de corps grew, even though in 1944 the division did not see action as a unit. That year those Cossack formations serving in the west were also sent to Yugoslavia and placed under Generalmajor von Pannwitz's command, bolstering his division's complement of heavy weapons. Von Pannwitz's unit was now much larger than a division. The 1st Cossack Cavalry Division became the XVth Cossack Cavalry Corps with two cavalry divisions and an infantry brigade. Von Pannwitz was named commanding general on February 1, 1945. The corps' mission in March 1945 was twofold:

1. Hold northward-facing defensive positions at the Drau River.
2. Offensive operations against the Yugoslavian People's Army in the Papuk Mountains.

With the war winding down, virtually the entire the XVth Cossack Cavalry Corps withdrew into the English-occupied part of Austria and surrendered there. However, the cossacks, their families and the German support personnel found no sanctuary there. In spite of promises made by the English, beginning on May 28, 1945 they were forcibly handed over to the Soviet Union. While the simple cossack troopers received the relatively mild punishment of eight years at forced labor and the German support personnel twenty-five years, the Supreme Military Court of the USSR sentenced General von Pannwitz and an unknown number of senior cossack commanders to death by hanging.

In conclusion, it is historically interesting to note that the German Reich employed seven cavalry divisions in action during the Second World War; if one includes the former 1st Cavalry Division, which became the 24th Panzer Division, the number of large cavalry units was eight.

In the First World War, during which motorization of the army played no significant role, the German Army had available eleven cavalry divisions, only three more than in the Second World War.

The regimental standard of Cavalry Regiment Center, which served on the Eastern Front. The regiment was created from "Cavalry Unit Boeselager" in 1943.

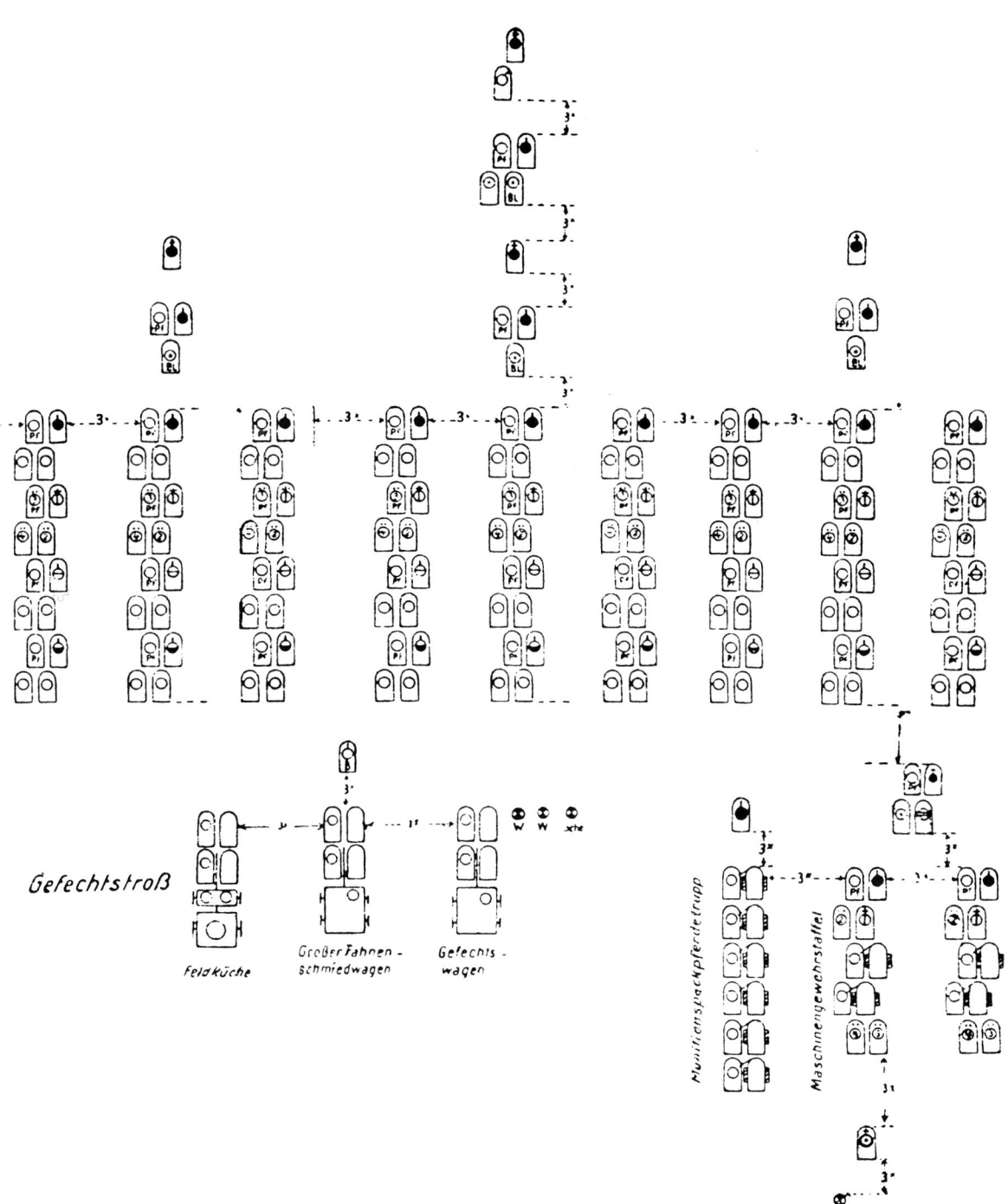

Gefechtstroß

Feldküche   GroßerFahnen-   Gefechts-
                   schmiedwagen   wagen

Munitionspackpferdetrupp

Maschinengewehrstaffel

The Bicycle Troop

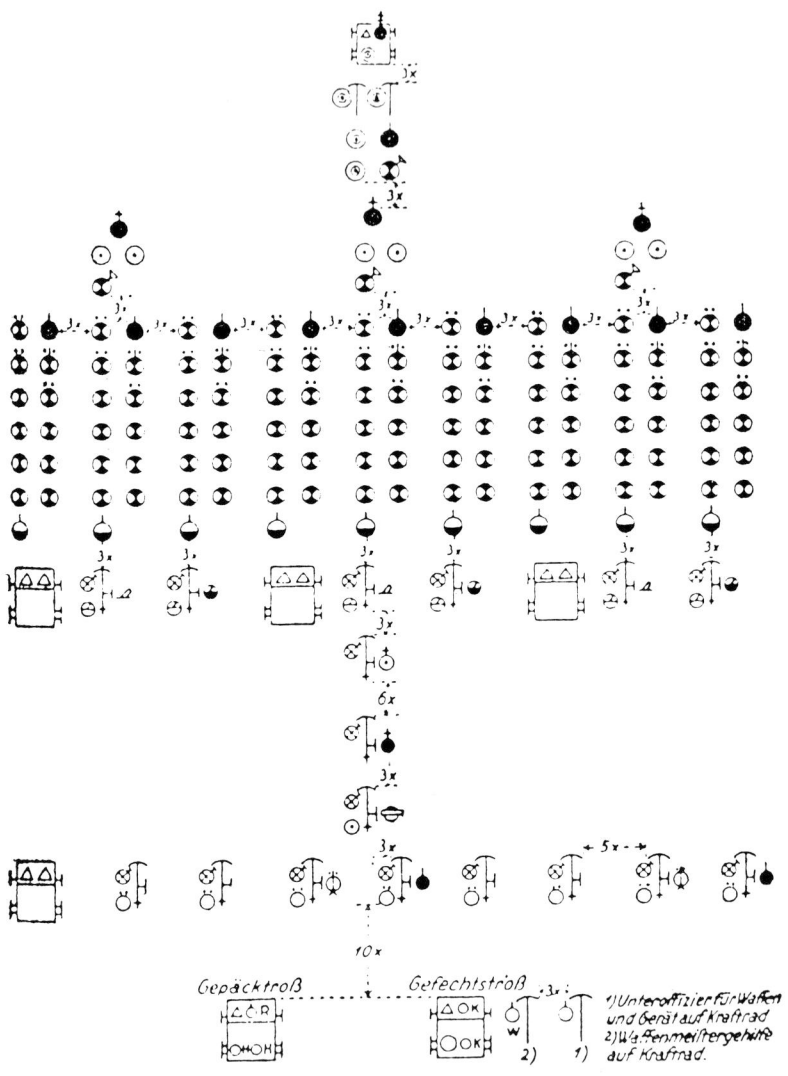

Gepäcktroß   Gefechtstroß

1) Unteroffizier für Waffen und Gerät auf Kraftrad
2) Wfg. Feinmeistergehilfe auf Kraftrad.

List of Symbols:

Troop commander
Platoon leader, section leader
Master sergeant
Squad leader, machine-gun squad leader, detail leader (troop headquarters detail)
Detail leader
Enlisted man
Bugler
Messenger (troop headquarters detail)
Messenger (platoon headquarters detail)
Commander – light machine-gun
Gunner – light machine-gun

Commander – mortar team
Gunner – mortar team
Accountant and Pay NCO
Rations officer
Cook
Mechanic
Motorcycle
Motorcycle and sidecar
All-terrain car

Commander – heavy machine-gun
Gunner – heavy machine-gun
Range-finder operator
Motorcycle driver
Motorcycle driver and escort

All-terrain truck
All-terrain truck with field range (cooker)

32

Part of the cavalry's ongoing training was the march. This photo was taken during Gruppenkommando 2's large-scale autumn maneuvers in 1936, which involved the Vth and IXth Army Corps. The sergeant in the foreground is wearing a sidearm which he inherited rather than the standard issue saber; this practice was authorized under certain circumstances.

UNIFORMS AND EQUIPMENT

Right:
Officer with cavalry helmet. This helmet, whose official service designation was "steel helmet with ear cutouts," helped to visually distinguished the cavalry from other branches of the service. However, the helmet was also worn by elements of the artillery and the signals corps.

Below:
5th Cavalry Regiment, Stolp, Pomerania. The troopers all wear the steel helmet with ear cutouts. In the background a barracks block of the former "Blücher Hussars."

Autumn maneuvers by the VIth Army Corps on the
Lüneburg Heath in 1935. Seen here is a parade by
the 15th Horse (later 15th Cavalry) Regiment based
at Paderborn, following the conclusion of maneuvers. Attached to the right side of the saddle behind
the riders are the leather pouches which contained
their mess kits.

Below and right:
Standard items of equipment for the trooper were
leather riding boots and spurs with buckle and
strap attachment.

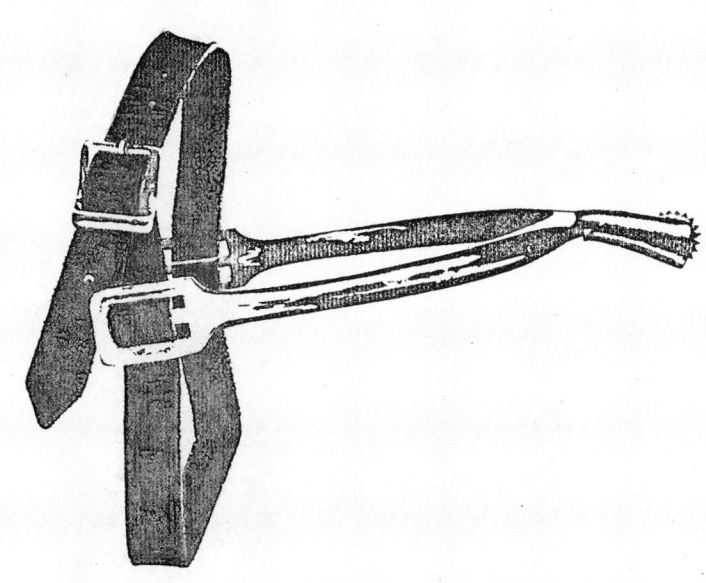

Right:
Worn with the riding boots were riding breeches with leather trim. Enlisted men also wore denim fatigue jackets while on work details.

Below:
The leather trim of the riding pants extended to below the knee in the front. Troopers of the 18th Cavalry Regiment, Cannstadt, while practicing the "grip with extended rifle sling," which was only done with the Karabiner 98b and 98k.

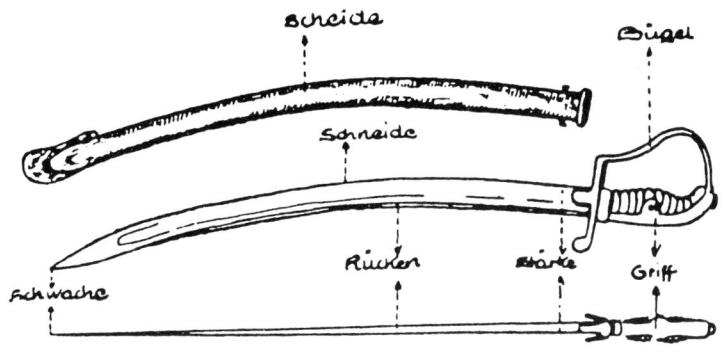

The enlisted man's saber, a weapon which was used exclusively by horse-mounted troops. Riflemen carried the weapon in a scabbard hung on the right side of the saddle behind the rider.

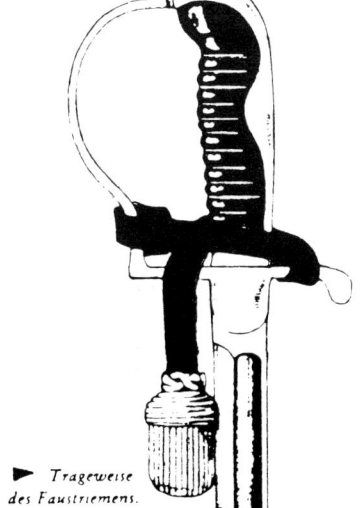

Above:
The enlisted man's saber as used by the Reichswehr and the Wehrmacht.

Right:
Method of attachment of the sword knot.

► *Trageweise des Faustriemens.*

Use of the officer's saber during a parade. Here the troop commander is issuing a command.

Standard equipment of the trooper until 1940; in this case however the saddle pack and saddle bags are absent.

Above left:
The saber was also worn with dress uniform. The pocketless tunic with Brandenburg cuffs was introduced on June 29, 1935. It soon came to be known in soldier's jargon as the "Kaiser Wilhelm memorial tunic" or the "Sarrasani," the latter referring to a well-known circus of the day.

Above:
Until the issue of the new tunic, service tunics were also worn as dress uniform. Prior to October 1, 1936 a Gefreiter (Lance Corporal) wore two chevrons.

Left:
The extra tunic was not just a part of the dress uniform, however. It was also worn on special occasions on horse as well as on foot.

Trooper of the 6th Cavalry Regiment, Darmstadt, 1938, in parade uniform with Kar 98k carbine, bayonet and enlisted man's saber. Note the saddle pad in place of the standard wool saddle blanket and the absence of saddle-bags.

Cavalry bivouac 1938. The rifles have been stacked, with saddles and other riding equipment laid out in front of them. On the right are two watering bags, which were made of duck cloth (water-proof canvas).

Equipment inspection. 6th Cavalry Regiment, Darmstadt, 1938.

Officers and sergeants carried the saber on the left side of the saddle. The white cap bands identify the two sergeants as assistant directors/umpires during maneuvers.

In the German cavalry much time was dedicated to caring for the horses. Consequently, many troopers felt more like a grooms than soldiers. Denim fatigue uniforms were standard attire.

While tending to the horses, this group of enlisted men wears the Reichsheer garrison cap; it was a folding cap similar to the service cap, but flexible so that it could be stuck into a pocket. The service caps worn by the sergeants and NCOs are still of the so-called "dinner plate shape."

Stable watch, 5th Cavalry Regiment, Stolp, Pomerania. The enlisted men are wearing the garrison cap for non-commissioned officers and enlisted men introduced in 1934, initial form. Nevertheless, the national emblem and the death's head of the former Danzig Bodyguard Hussars are already evident.

Members of an officer training course held at the Krampnitz Cavalry School (near Potsdam) from October 1939 to January 1940. The course participants are wearing the service uniform with saber, the course director a greatcoat. The coat, made of a finer cloth in a lighter, silver-gray color, was worn as a "personal coat" by officers of the Reichsheer. Procurement ended on March 31, 1938. As it was strongly reminiscent of the overcoats of the old army, it received the unofficial designation "loyal to the emperor coat." It remained extremely popular even after procurement ended and in fact new garments continued to be made as long as there was fabric available. In the background is the so-called "Eagle Portal" of the first barracks built in Krampnitz in 1939.

Officers and sergeants, members of the headquarters of a reconnaissance battalion during the campaign in France in 1940. Note the different shades of material of the officer coats.

Standard troop of the 13th Cavalry Regiment, Lüneburg, on Heroes Memorial Day 1938. The two officers of the standard troop wear the "loyal to the emperor coat"; they and the officer in front wear the fill-dress sword belt introduced in 1937.

Mounted standard detachment of the 6th Cavalry Regiment, Darmstadt. Note the bandolier worn by the standard bearer.

Members of the 18th Cavalry Regiment taking the oath of allegiance on the regimental standard, Cannstadt. This photo was taken at the end of the 1930s and these cavalrymen still wear the M 18 steel helmet. The enlisted man's saber is worn slung on a strap suspended from the belt. Standard bearer with bandolier and gorget.

*Standard
(Artillery, cavalry and signals units, as well as the organic or independent battalions of all motorized or horse-drawn units)*

Generals and officers wore the saber "underslung" on a narrow belt and the outwardly-distinguishable "special scabbard carrier."

Left:
The officer's uniform included the waist belt and shoulder strap. The waist belt was closed by a rectangular buckle with twin prongs. The shoulder strap was deleted following the Polish Campaign in accordance with a decree issued on September 20, 1939. The officer on the right wears the insignia of an adjutant in the form of an aiguillette, as well as the garrison cap for officers (no cord or chin strap and without the national emblem), however with the "Swedte Eagle" of the 6th Cavalry Regiment. The officer on the left is wearing the so-called "saddle-shaped" peaked cap.

Right:
The garrison cap for officers (left) and the garrison cap for NCOs and enlisted men (right), second version with soutache (flat cotton braid in the appropriate service color).

Generalfeldmarschall von Brauchitsch, Commander in Chief of the Army, out for a morning ride with his adjutant. Clearly visible here, and on the bottom of Page 45, are the riding pants worn by generals, with bright red piping and trim stripes, which were referred to as Lampassen (an Austrian term for the trim stripes).

The uniform of the race rider. Horse racing, which was actively encouraged in the Wehrmacht, demanded the introduction of lightweight jackets in different colors for easier identification. No shoulder straps or collar patches were worn on these jackets, although a somewhat smaller version of the national emblem was retained. Each regiment active in racing, as well as individual branches of the service, commands, and schools, was assigned a specific color (see right). There were a total of 38 different racing colors in the army.

Army Riding and Driving School	antique gold
1st Horse Regiment	fawn
2nd Horse Regiment	water green
3rd Cavalry Regiment	wine red
4th Cavalry Regiment	blue
5th Cavalry Regiment	black
6th Cavalry Regiment	dark green
8th Cavalry Regiment	medium brown
9th Cavalry Regiment	cornflower blue
10th Cavalry Regiment	light leather
11th Cavalry Regiment	strawberry red
13th Cavalry Regiment	lemon yellow
14th Cavalry Regiment	blue-gray
15th Cavalry Regiment	garish green
17th Cavalry Regiment	grayish-green
18th Cavalry Regiment	lime
1st Artillery Regiment	dove-gray
4th Artillery Regiment	earth-gray
5th Artillery Regiment	gold-yellow
7th Artillery Regiment	leaf-green
10th Artillery Regiment	gray-brown
11th Artillery Regiment	rust
12th Artillery Regiment	steel-blue
15th Artillery Regiment	dark lilac
19th Artillery Regiment	navy blue
21st Artillery Regiment	beige
22nd Artillery Regiment	purple
23rd Artillery Regiment	red
26th Artillery Regiment	blue-violet
27th Artillery Regiment	blackberry
32nd Artillery Regiment	dusty rose
33rd Artillery Regiment	pale violet
96th Artillery Regiment	medium blue
98th Artillery Regiment	dark red
1st Horse Artillery Battalion	lilac
Supply Train Battalions	light blue
Infantry Regiments	white
Motorized Units and Signals Battalions	pink

An important item of equipment was the triangular Zeltbahn 31 (tent square or shelter half). Not only could it be used to construct large or small tents, it also served as camouflage and more significantly as a rain cape. Neither the Reichsheer nor the Wehrmacht had specialized waterproof garments.

Below:
Method of wearing the Zeltbahn 31 as a rain cape.

Above:
War artist and book illustrator Albert
Reich's impression of the cavalryman in
France in 1940.

Left:
Georg Sluytermann von Langeweyde
captured the cavalryman and his
equipment with scientific precision in
this contemporary woodcut.

Personnel of the 6th Reconnaissance Battalion (6th Westphalian Infantry Division) during the campaign against France in 1940. The photo illustrates the three main types of uniform worn by members of a "recon battalion": in the right background is a motorcyclist in the "protective coat for motorcyclists" (Kradmantel); in the center is a sergeant wearing riding boots and breeches with leather trim; and left the standard service uniform with marching boots (jackboots).

Below:
In many cases the equipment carried by the horse differed from the peacetime pack arrangement. This NCO has loaded his mount with a Packtasche 34 saddlebag together with rear as well as front saddle packs. In this instance there is a spade where the saber was formerly carried.

It was not uncommon during the war for horse troops to be converted into bicycle troops. Here one such troop is seen in East Prussia in 1941. The riding boots and breeches have been replaced by long pants, laced boots and gas masks.

Below: Members of the troop headquarters detail of the 2nd Horse Regiment's 5th Troop in Poland in 1939. Introduced in 1933, the battle-dress tunic was the most commonly-worn item of uniform during the Second World War. The turndown collar was worn open. Camouflage covers or nets were not introduced until 1942; however, this Obergefreiter (corporal) has fashioned his own camouflage cover for his helmet.

Officer of the 6th Cavalry Regiment, Darmstadt, in the battle-dress tunic for officers. This tailor-made tunic frequently exhibited deviations in color and cut from the standard laid down in the manuals. Here the peaked cap (with cordon) is worn like the garrison cap, the loosely-inserted spring steel ring having been removed. This was a popular practice, but one contrary to regulations. As was standard in the Wehrmacht, the mount is bridled with an S-type bit.

Right:
It was not unusual for personnel of motorized units to have to turn once again to the horse. The equipment worn by horse and rider was improvised and frequently the only mounts available were captured Russian panye horses. Rittmeister (cavalry captain) Schubert of the 36th Motorized Reconnaissance Battalion in Russia, 1942.

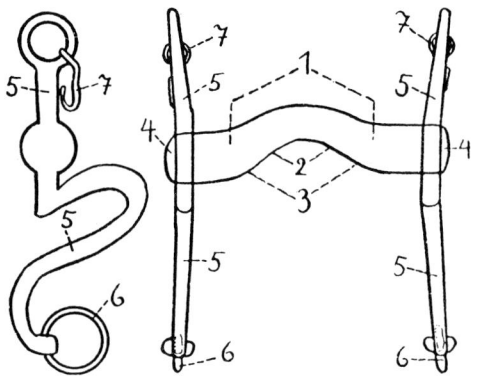

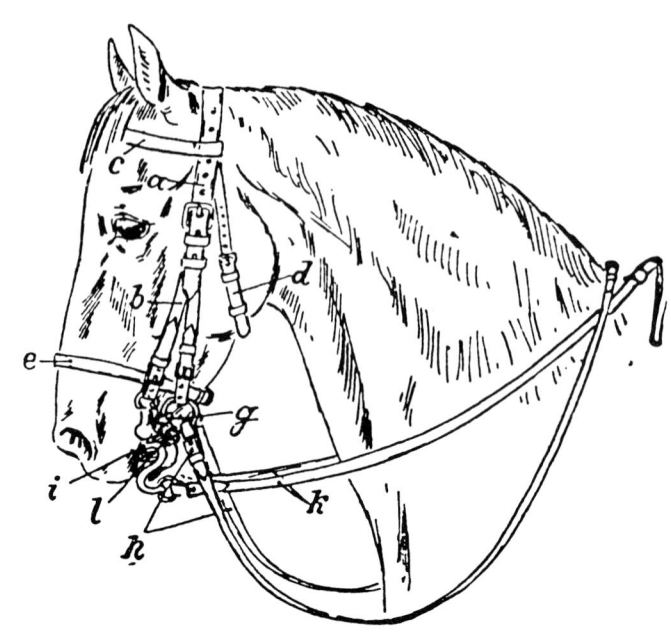

1. Mouthpiece
2. Free space for horse's tongue
3. Heel
4. Cap
5. Side piece
6. Rein ring
7. Curb chain hook

Below: Non-commissioned officers of the 5th Troop of the 22nd Horse Regiment (1st Cavalry Division) following the campaign in Holland. The "piston rings" denoting the troop sergeant adorn the sleeve of the Unterwachtmeister (staff sergeant); the two NCOs in the center of the photo have outfitted themselves with raincoats from captured stocks.

After the Western Campaign in 1940, German forces began practicing for Operation Seelöwe (Sea Lion), the proposed landing in England. Part of a reconnaissance battalion in Belgium during these maneuvers. The officer in the center of the photo is wearing a Type 35 message blank pouch, the version with leather buckle.

Left:
Typical uniform worn by the cavalry officer during the war, here with experimental restyled garrison cap in Russia, 1941.

Right:
A Rittmeister (cavalry captain) of the former 18th Cavalry Regiment during the campaign in Russia. Visible on the garrison cap is the national emblem, which was contrary to service regulations.

Left:
Photographed in Russia, this horseman is still equipped with the Packtasche 34 saddlebags (installed on the front of the saddle). The carbine scabbard carrier has already been dropped. The horse wears a halter headstall in addition to the bridle, in order to allow the rider to tie up his mount at any time. Probably a dispatch rider.

Left:
A cavalry officer, barely identifiable as such, in the winter of 1942-43. He wears an overcoat which extends to approximately 10 centimeters above the ankles. Type 35 message blank pouch with metal-edged fastener. The cavalryman in the background is wearing the cloth overcoat.

Below:
Cavalrymen of the newly-created Cavalry Regiment Center (K.R.M.) in the early summer of 1943 during a training demonstration. With the exception of the camouflage cover for the Type 35 steel helmet, uniforms and equipment have changed little since the start of the war against Russia.

Left:
Generalfeldmarschall von Kluge and Major von Boeselager review an honor guard of personnel from Cavalry Regiment Center. The reappearance of army cavalry units in the fifth year of the war was due to the combined efforts of these two officers. The photo provides an especially good view of the "belt carrying fixture for cavalry"; it was officially introduced on February 15, 1940 under the designation "carrying belt for ammunition pouches."

Right:
The field uniform of an Oberwachtmeister (master sergeant) of the 32nd Horse Regiment in Russia in September 1944.

Not until after the considerable losses to frostbite in the winter of 1941-42 in Russia was winter clothing introduced for the army, and it wasn't until autumn 1942 that it was issued to the troops in quantity. The horseman and the gunners wear the padded winter jacket with hood, which extended roughly to mid-thigh. The jacket and the pants that went with it could be worn over the uniform as outer clothing.

Until the winter of 1941 the cloth greatcoat was the soldier's only significant protection against the cold; however, it was inadequate for the rigors of a northern winter. Here an infantry horse platoon with the snow-covered mountains of Norway in the background, spring 1940.

THE BUGLER CORPS

The peacetime budget allocated a bugler corps to each horse-mounted or horse-drawn unit. A Wehrmacht bugler corps consisted of 28 men: 1 bandmaster (officer rank), 26 brass-wind players and 1 drummer. In the photograph is the bugler corps of the 15th Horse Regiment, Paderborn, on the occasion of the field parade following the VIth Army Corps' autumn maneuvers on the Lüneburg Heath in 1935.

The distinguishing feature of soldiers in the music service were the so-called "Swallow's Nests," which were worn with the service coat as well as the battledress tunic. The bugler corps of the 7th Horse Regiment, Breslau, in service coats. The bandmaster is not wearing "swallow's nests."

Kettledrummer, bandmaster and buglers of the 13th Cavalry Regiment, Lüneburg Schlieffen Barracks while preparing to set out on a St. Hubert's Day hunt. Some horse-mounted and horse-drawn units had a pack of English foxhounds for practicing the hunt.

The drum draperies correspond to the type introduced in 1937.

Left:
Kettledrummer of the 8th Cavalry Regiment, Oels, Silesia. Use of the traditional drum draperies of units of the old army was banned after 1937.

Kettledrummers and ceremonial trumpet group on the occasion of an equestrian display in the Deutschlandhalle in Berlin. The ceremonial trumpets were supplementary instruments adorned with fanfare flags, the design of which was largely left to the units. The drummer controlled his mount with his feet by means of snaffle reins, which passed through curb reins behind the harness buckle.

The bugler corps were supposed to be disbanded once mobilization began; however this was not carried out in all cases. Disbandment resulted in the buglers being assigned to newly-established battalions and troops. Those bugler corps that survived or were reformed ceased wearing the "swallow's nests" after the campaign in France.

The bugler was an important means of command in the hands of the troop commander. The signal trumpet was never officially retired during the war, although it was scarcely ever used.

The German Cavalry Newspaper was the organ of former and active cavalrymen until into the second half of the war. The emphasis of the paper was the maintenance of long-standing cavalry traditions.

Conclusion of a maneuver by the 2nd Horse Regiment (1st Cavalry Division) in Poland, spring 1941. On the extreme left of the photo two buglers blow the signal "full stop!"

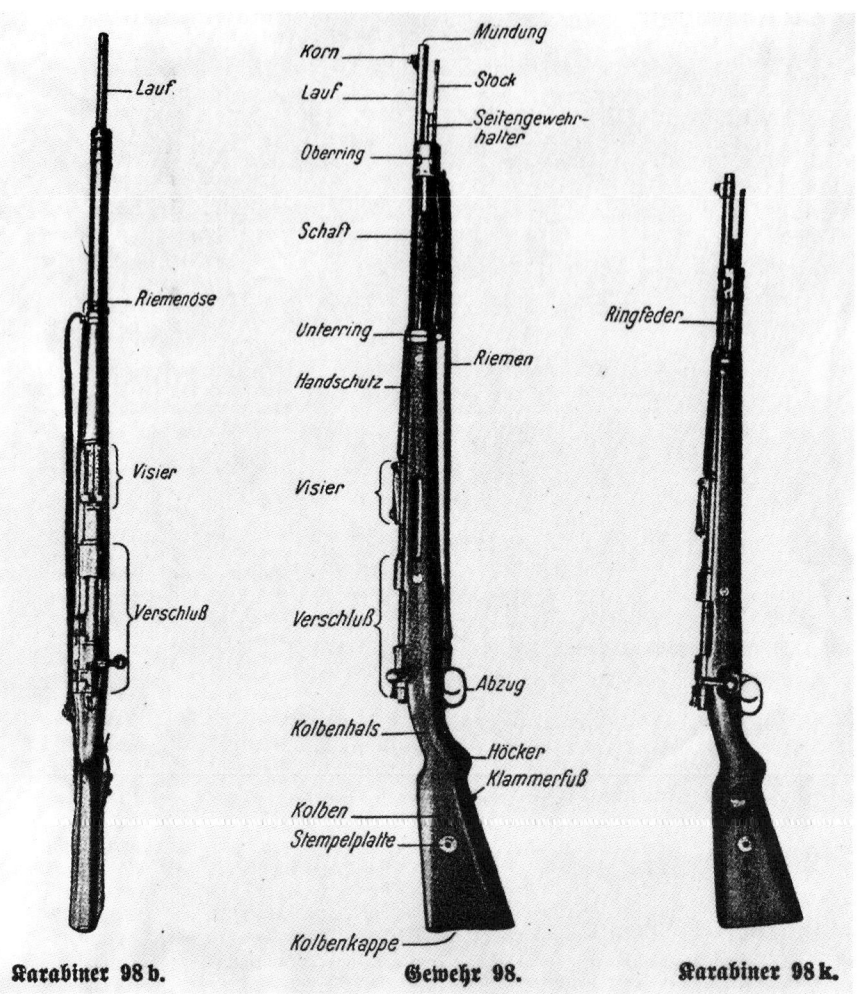

Karabiner 98 b.   Gewehr 98.   Karabiner 98 k.

The cavalry of the old army was equipped with the Karabiner 98a, whose performance was inferior to that of the infantry rifle. As the cavalry of the Reichsheer was supposed to be a "fast firearm-equipped force," introduction of the Karabiner 98b was necessary. The latter differed from the Gewehr 98 only in having a curved bolt handle and side-mounted sling loops. The weapon's length made it unsatisfactory for use by horse-mounted troops, however, and the Karabiner 98k was introduced in 1935. This weapon proved extraordinarily successful and became the standard weapon of the German Armed Forces.

The regimental commander of the 15th Horse Regiment, Paderborn, taking target practice with the Kar 98b. Clearly visible are the side-mounted sling loops.

The Karabiner 98b was carried in a carbine scabbard on the left side of the saddle.

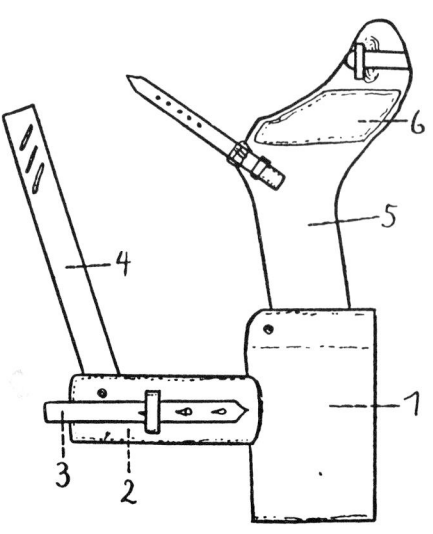

Like the Kar 98a, the Karabiner 98b was initially carried slung over the rider's back. As the rifle projected well above the rider due on account of its length, there were a number of serious accidents involving low-hanging branches. Introduction of the rifle scabbard carrier largely eliminated this problem.

Rifle Scabbard Carrier

1. *Boot*
2. *Web*
3. *Keeper*
4. *Turnback*
5. *Fastening strap*
6. *Wooden block (leather-covered, to keep rifle away from surface of saddle)*

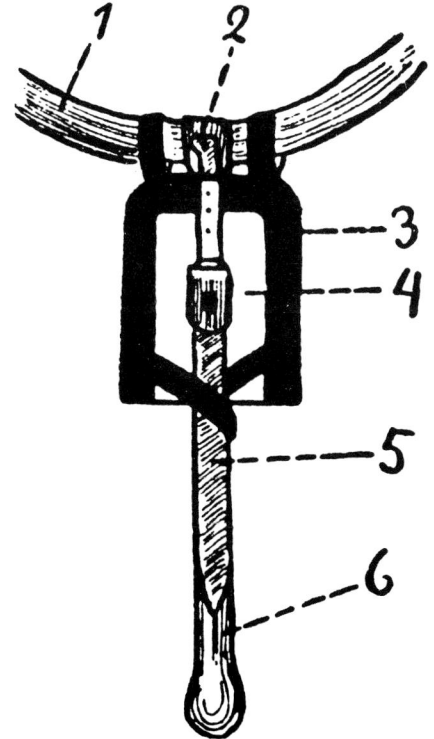

The Karabiner 98k was introduced into service beginning in 1935. Here a horseman of the 15th Cavalry Regiment during combat training. The photo provides a good view of the "small entrenching tool," spade with buckle-attached bayonet.

Small Entrenching Tool

1. **Belt**
2. **Bayonet scabbard**
3. **Spade sheath**
4. **Spade blade**
5. **Bayonet**
6. **Short spade handle**

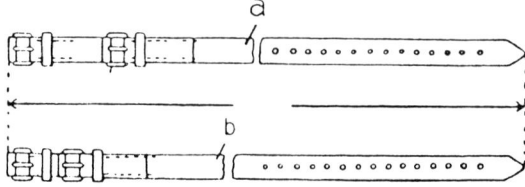

Type 25 army saddle with Packtasche 34 saddlebags, rear saddle pack and carbine scabbard carrier, which was also used to carry the Kar 98k until the end of 1940.

The saddle, which included three pack straps, was held in place by the girth.

Die Packriemen, zwei Seitenpackriemen (a) und ein Mittelpackriemen (b), bestehen aus je einem Schnallriemen mit Schlaufe, die am Stößelende noch mit einem zweiten, besonders aufgenähten Schnallstößel mit Schlaufe versehen sind.

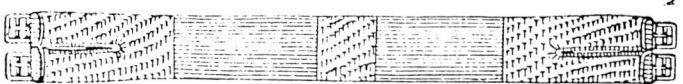

Sattelgurt.

Schnurensattelgurt ohne Schnallstößel.

Der Schnurensattelgurt, aus 22 Hanfschnuren, wird in vier Größennummern gefertigt. Die Schnallen sind eingeflochten; zwischen Schnallen und

Schnuren.

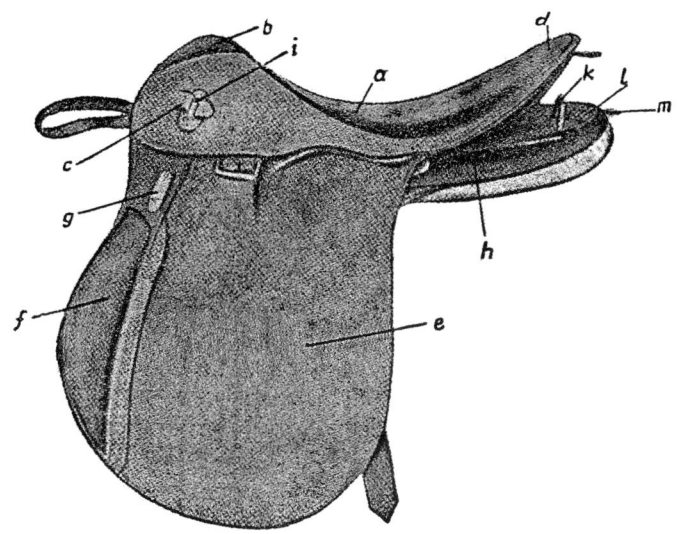

Type 25 Army Saddle

a. saddle seat
b. leather cap
c. notch with pommel-pad strap
d. metal slot for middle pack strap
e. skirt
f. knee pad

g. fitting for the saddlebag
h. saddle pad
i. buckle for the martingale strap
k. pack ring
l. fitting for the breeching strap
m. leather piece for tightening buckle

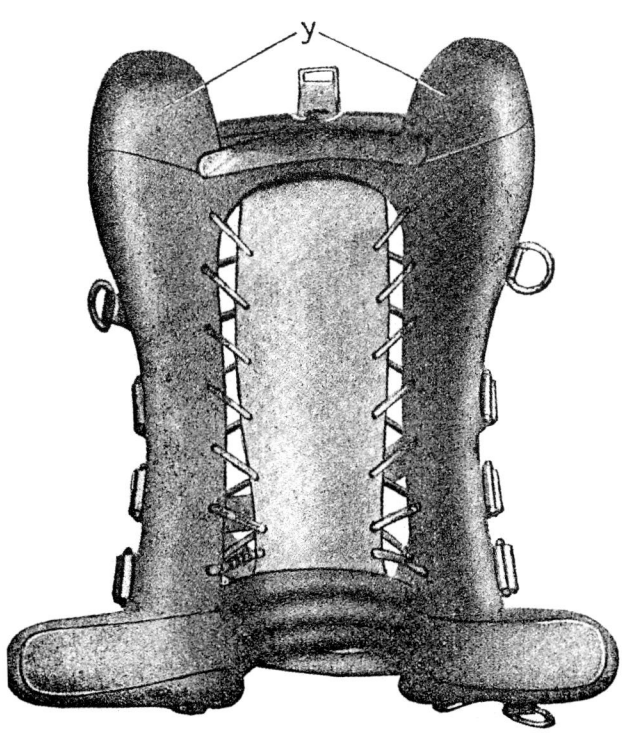

The good, horse-sparing sit of the Type 25 army saddle was due to its new-type saddletree.

The Versailles Treaty allowed each Reichsheer cavalry regiment one machine-gun platoon with four heavy machine-guns. The platoon headquarters personnel, gun commander and driver (from the saddle) were equipped as horse-mounted soldiers.

The sMG 08 (water-cooled) heavy machine-gun could be mounted on a Type 16 tripod or on a sleigh mount. Mounting the weapon on the sleigh mount increased range and accuracy.

For transport the sMG 08 was packed onto a Machine-gun Wagon 08, which was pulled by a six-horse team. The gunners who rode on the wagon were dressed the same as infantry. The water-cooled sMG 08 remained in Wehrmacht service until the introduction of the MG 34.

In this photo the gunners still carry the Karabiner 98a as their personal weapon; retired by the army, the Kar 98a continued to be used by the police.

The Reichsheer cavalry was later permitted a light version of the weapon with no tripod or sleigh mount, the lMG 08/15, for use as a section machine-gun, and it continued in use with the Wehrmacht. The 1st machine-gunner carried the "light" machine-gun with him in a scabbard on the left side of his saddle. A box of machine-gun ammunition on the right side provided a counterweight. See the horseman in the foreground.

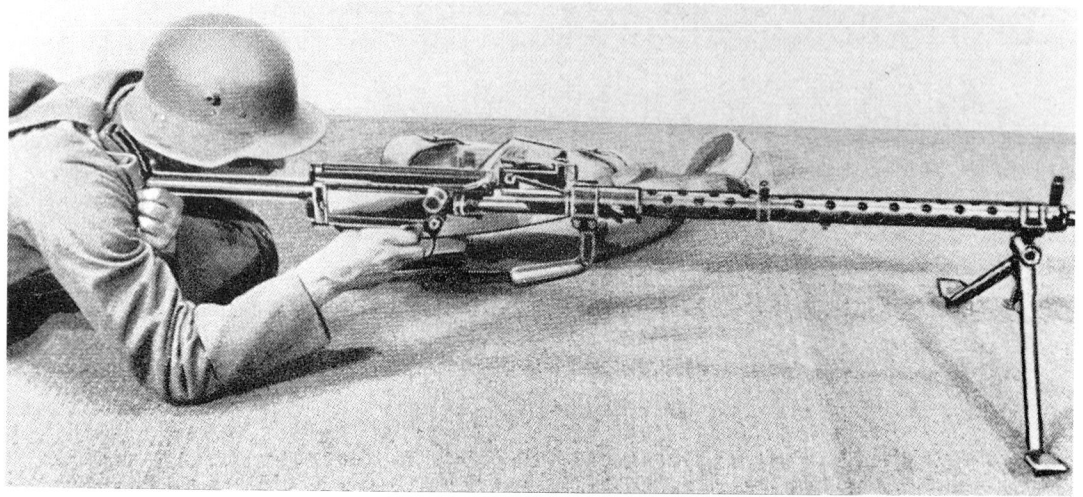

Above and below:
The lMG 13 (Dreyse) light machine-gun used by the Reichsheer was also introduced into the cavalry in the mid-1930s – later with a long flash suppressor. It could be used with a bipod or on an adjustable tripod. There was no gun mount for this weapon.

Machine-gun half-squad. The lMG 13 (Dreyse) is mounted on the left side of the 1st machine-gunner's saddle behind the rider.

Dismounting for combat. Following the introduction of the MG 34 the tripod remained in use in the anti-aircraft role and was carried on the back, as here by the headquarters personnel of a machine-gun platoon.

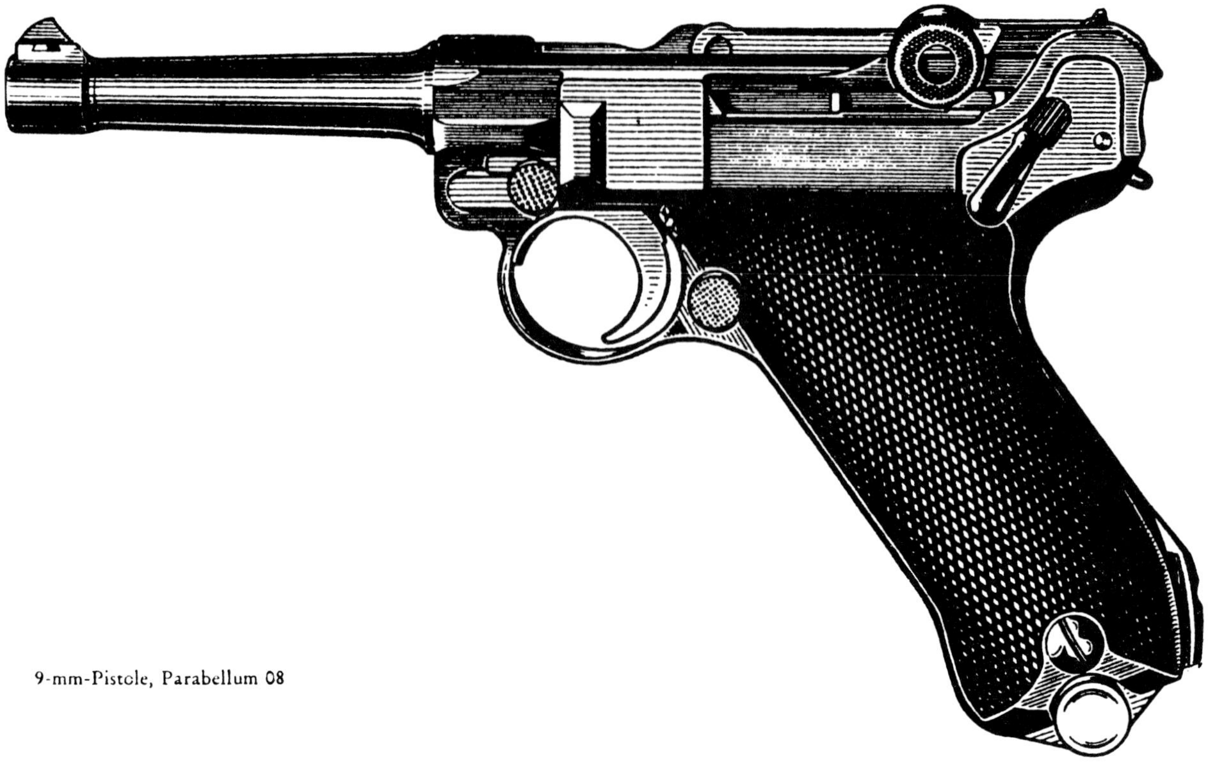

9-mm-Pistole, Parabellum 08

The Pistole 08 served as a personal weapon for officers, troop sergeants and medical personnel. For whatever reasons, the Pistole 38, which succeeded the P 08, saw only limited use.

Carriage of the holster for the Pistole 08. The battledress tunic and belt of the officer in the foreground do not exactly fit as per regulations. Right: Generalmajor Feldt, commanding officer of the 1st Cavalry Division.

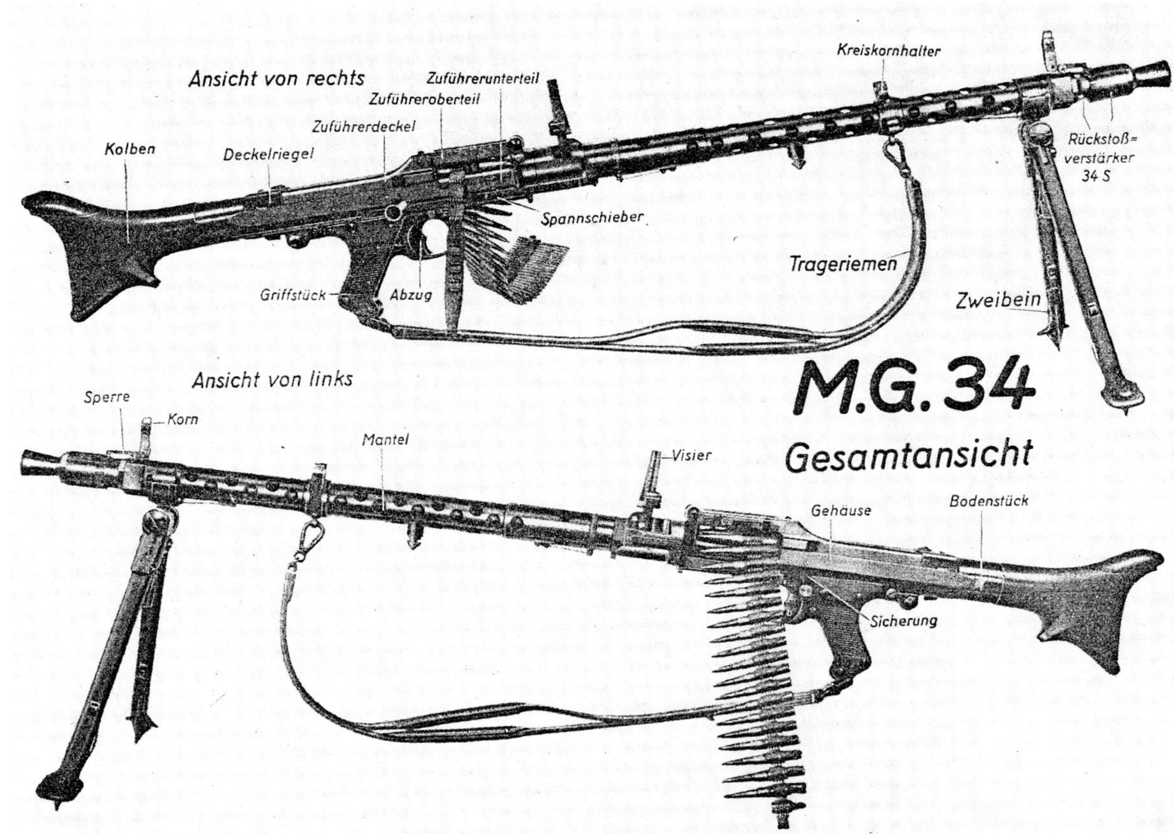

Ansicht von rechts

Kolben
Deckelriegel
Zuführerdeckel
Zuführeroberteil
Zuführerunterteil
Kreiskornhalter
Rückstoß= verstärker 34 S
Spannschieber
Griffstück
Abzug
Trageriemen
Zweibein

M.G. 34
Gesamtansicht

Ansicht von links

Sperre
Korn
Mantel
Visier
Gehäuse
Bodenstück
Sicherung

Developed from the MG 13 (Dreyse), the MG 34 was the first modern machine-gun, although the weapon still possessed some minor shortcomings. The MG 34 could be used with a gun mount as a heavy machine-gun or with a bipod as a light machine-gun.

Only after it was equipped with the MG 34 did the cavalry truly become a "fast firearm-equipped force." Each horse and bicycle troop had at its disposal nine light and two (later four) heavy machine-guns. The machine-gun thus became the main combat weapon of the horsemen as it was of the infantry.

The fire of the heavy machine-guns was directed by the platoon headquarters personnel and was roughly comparable to the fire direction of other heavy weapons. The officer in the foreground is wearing "personal riding boots," with which the spurs were usually worn just below the ankle.

The bicycle troop, the infantry element of the partly-motorized reconnaissance battalion, was equipped with three 50-mm mortars. Beyond the mortar is the carrying case for the mortar shells.

Shortly before the start of the war all non-commissioned officers responsible for command functions were equipped with the MPi 38 submachine-gun (approximately 15 per troop). This represented a considerable increase in firepower, especially at short and medium ranges. Two Wachtmeister (sergeants) of the 2nd Horse Regiment in Russia in 1941. They both carry the P 08 pistol in addition to the submachine-gun.

77

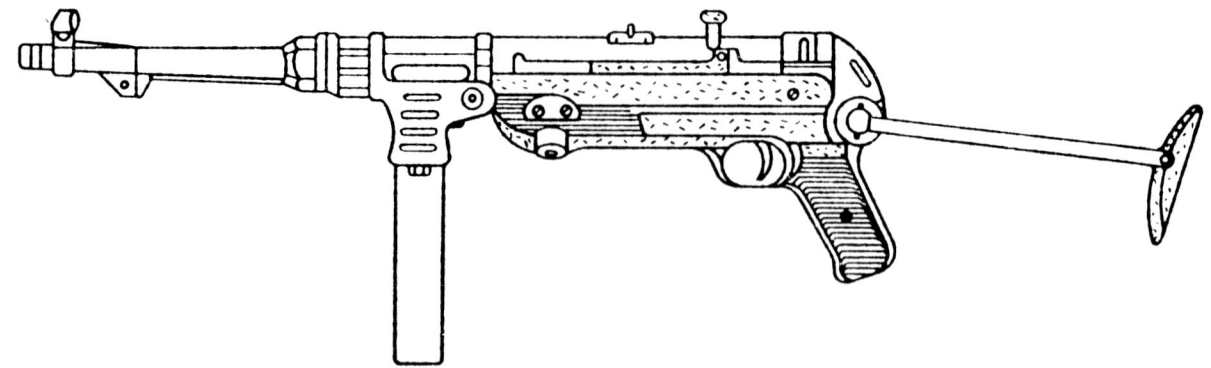

MP 40 Submachine-gun

For the most part the horse-mounted units of the Waffen-SS were equipped like those of the army. Here a section leader carries the MPi 40 (later version of the MPi 38) slung across his chest. Beneath the right saddlebag is the so-called water bag made of waterproof duck cloth. Russia 1941.

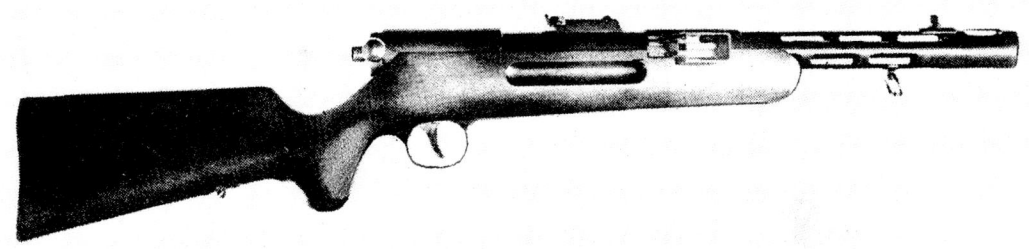

The Army and Waffen-SS
used various other types of
submachine-guns in
addition to the MPi 40.
Illustrated above is the
Erma (MPi 34)
submachine-gun, which is
also being carried by the
radio operator.

The MG 34 was also a standard weapon of the Waffen-SS cavalry; here ammunition is being fed from a drum magazine.

As wheeled motor vehicles usually lacked a machine-gun mount, in many cases the anti-aircraft tripod had to fill that function in a makeshift way. SS Cavalry Division (later the 8th SS Cavalry Division) in Russia in 1942.

The anti-aircraft tripod, which originally accompanied every MG 34, was not just used in the anti-aircraft role. In terrain with tall ground foliage, as for example in the sunflower fields of Southern Russia, it provided the only means of using the weapon effectively. 8th SS Cavalry Division Florian Geyer at the Dniepr River in 1943.

The MG 42.

Formed from the 17th SS Horse Regiment in early 1944, the SS Volunteer Cavalry Divison Maria Theresia was partially equipped with the new MG 42. March 1944 in the Kovel pocket.

Panzerbüchse PzB 38 und PzB 39, Kal. 7,92 mm

The Panzerbüchse 39 anti-tank rifle. It was only seldom used by the cavalry.

August 1944. Rail transport of units of the 22nd Volunteer Cavalry Division Maria Theresia into the Transylvania region of Romania. The Kar 98k carbine and the MG 34 machine-gun (foreground) remained the standard weapons of the horse-mounted troops.

The Horse Troop

Outwardly, the horse troop changed little following the retirement of the steel lance in 1927. The "steel helmet with ear cutouts" was worn until the end of the 1930s. However, with the introduction of the Kar 98b carbine, the horse-mounted soldier could fight dismounted on foot in the same way as the infantryman. The motorcycle dispatch rider attached to each troop significantly improved communications between the troop and the regiment.
3rd Horse Regiment, Rathenow and Stendal, during the IXth Army's autumn maneuvers in Bavaria, 1935.

This painting by soldier-artist Döbrich-Steglitz depicts a scene typical of a horse troop in combat. The approach on horseback, dismounting in cover, the advance by the dismounted cavalry riflemen and the horses being led away.

The 5th Cavalry Regiment based as Stolp, Pomerania returning from a maneuver in 1937. Illustrated here is the regiment's machine-gun troop. The rider on the extreme right edge of the photo carries one Type 34 ammunition box for machine-gun in a case on the left side of his saddle; the trooper in the right center has a Type 14 (34) range-finder slung across his back. The rolled-up tent square has been placed under the rear of the saddle for better carriage.

Horse-mounted troops ride deployed in terrain.

Number	Signal	Execution	Color	Meaning
1		Raise arm (a) by officer (with whistle blast) b) by NCO – (c) While on the move (mounted) –	white	(a) "Attention!" (signals an announcement) (b) "Understood" or "Ready to move out!" (c) "Sit still!"
2		Raise arm once, repeat several times (a) while stopped (b) While on the move	white green green	"Mount up!" (a) "Move out, move off (motor vehicle)!" (b) "Next higher gear, faster!"

Command of horse-mounted and horse-drawn units was largely by means of hand signals; twenty-five standard hand signals were provided, two of which are illustrated below.

In some cases the enlisted man's saber was used by horse-mounted troops until mid-1941 and was carried "sabers up!" on special occasions. The 5th Cavalry Regiment, Stolp, in parade formation in 1936.

A horse platoon during a parade with "eyes right!" and "sabers up!"

The saber was not just for parades, however. A horse troop of the 15th Cavalry Regiment, Paderborn and Neuhaus, practices the attack at the Sennelager Troop Training Grounds.

A mounted patrol consisting of one NCO and three enlisted men reconnoiters toward the Narew River. Poland 1939.

Typical equipment of a horse-mounted troop. Horsemen of the 15th Cavalry Regiment enroute to the Hahn-Weide Troop Training Grounds in 1938.

Officers and sergeants carried the saber on the left side of the saddle. As a rule officers did not carry saddlebags. A horse regiment during the German entry into the Sudetenland in 1938.

The 1st machine-gunner of a cavalry section removing a lMG 34 from its scabbard. The saddlebag on the front of the saddle contains a box of ammunition for the MG 34.

Salute with the saber! Normally done only by officers in the army, in the Waffen-SS also by senior non-commissioned officers in positions of command.

Three Gefreiter (lance corporals) of the 34th Infantry Horse Platoon (34th Infantry Regiment), Heilbronn. Their equipment –riding boots, spurs, breeches with leather trim – is the same as that of the horse-mounted troops of horse or cavalry regiments.

The leading elements of the 1st Cavalry Division reach the west coast of Holland on May 16, 1940.

Riding Horse

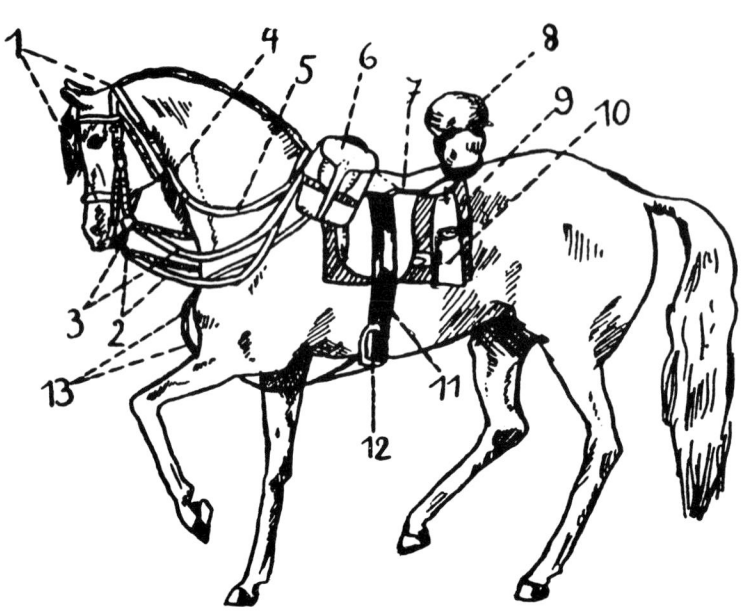

1. Bridle
2. Curb bit with curb rein
3. Snaffle with snaffle rein
4. Halter
5. Halter strap
6. Saddlebag
7. Saddle
8. Rider forage pack, tarpaulin, coat
9. Saddle blanket
10. Rifle scabbard carrier
11. Surcingle
12. Stirrup with stirrup strap
13. Martingale

Standard equipment of the riding horse.

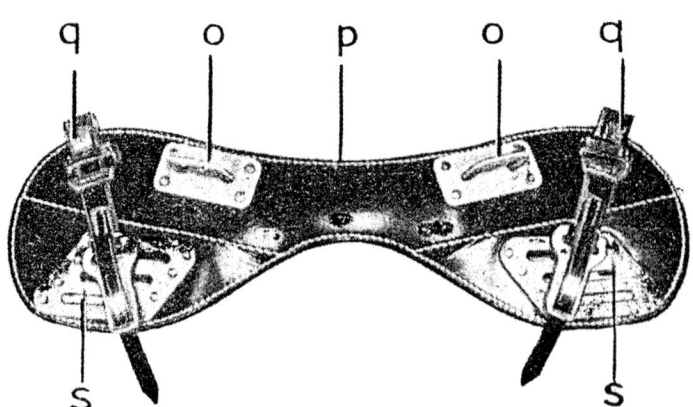

(c) The saddle overthrow is cut from browned cowhide in a curved, wing-like shape, doubled with a second layer of sleeked leather on the underside to the level of the aperture, and reinforced throughout with inner or under layers of transparent leather. The overthrow is pressed to sit flat on the saddle.

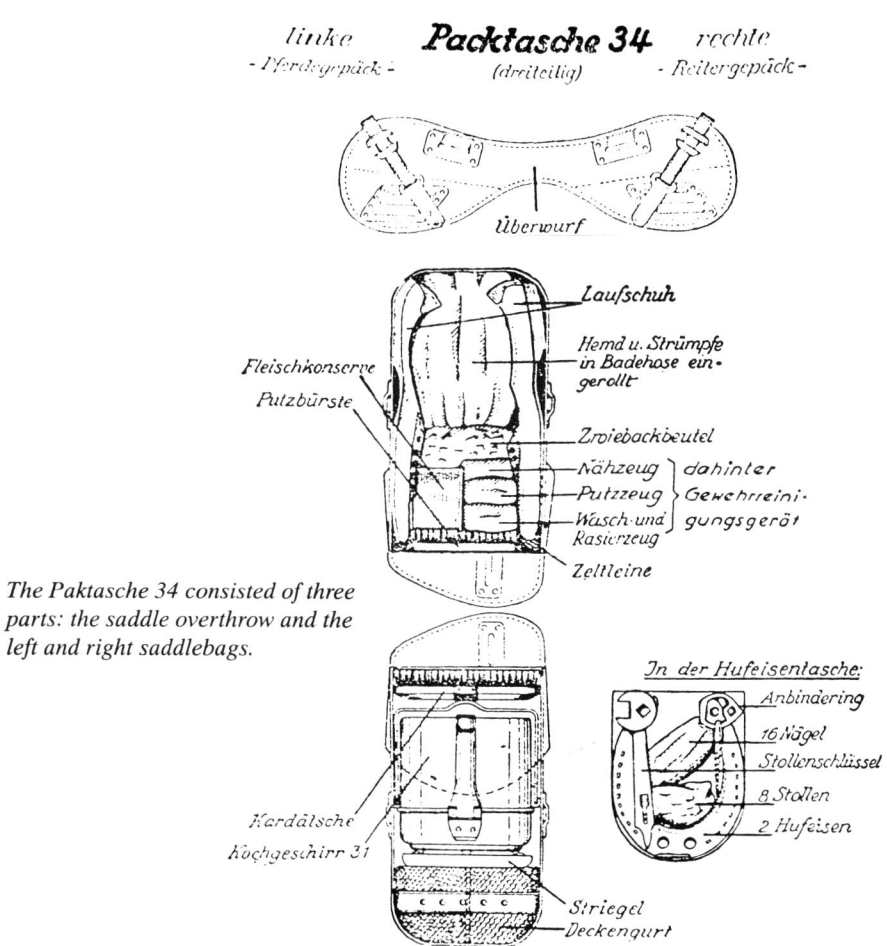

linke *Packtasche 34* **rechte**
- *Pferdegepäck* - *(dreiteilig)* - *Reitergepäck* -

Überwurf

Laufschuh

Hemd u. Strümpfe in Badehose eingerollt

Fleischkonserve

Putzbürste

Zwiebackbeutel

Nähzeug
Putzzeug
Wasch- und Rasierzeug
} *dahinter Gewehrreinigungsgerät*

Zeltleine

The Paktasche 34 consisted of three parts: the saddle overthrow and the left and right saddlebags.

In der Hufeisentasche:

Anbindering

16 Nägel

Stollenschlüssel

8 Stollen

2 Hufeisen

Kardätsche

Hochgeschirr 31

Striegel

Deckengurt

Horse troop of the 1st Cavalry Division in France, 1940. In action the Kar 98k was frequently carried slung across the rider's back.

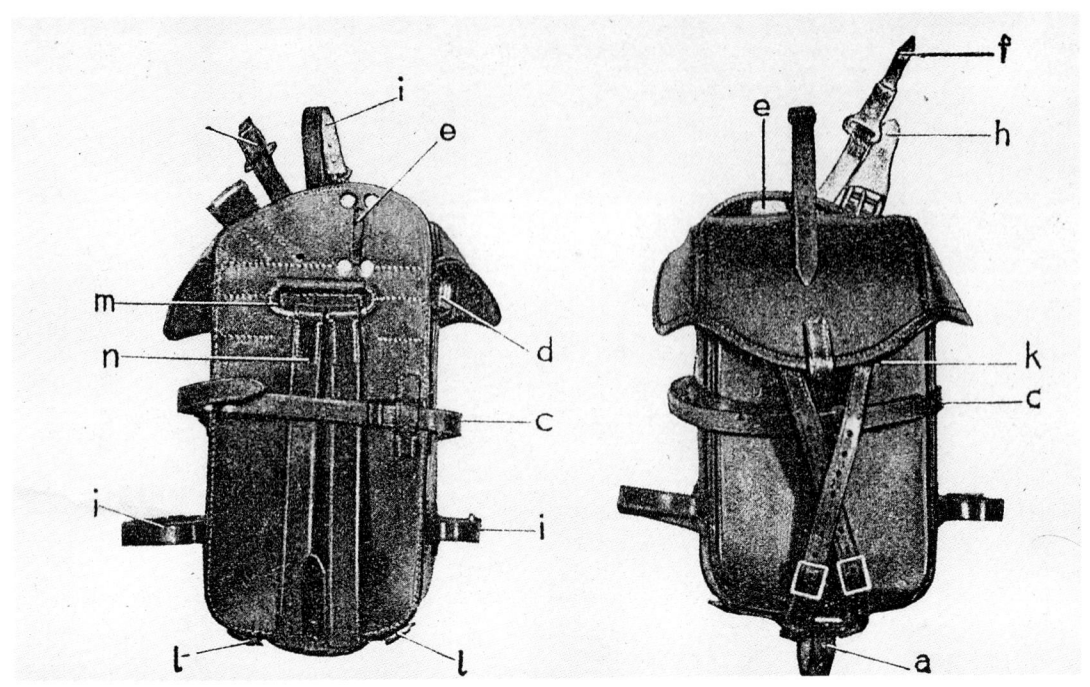

Right (above) and left Packtasche 34 saddlebags.

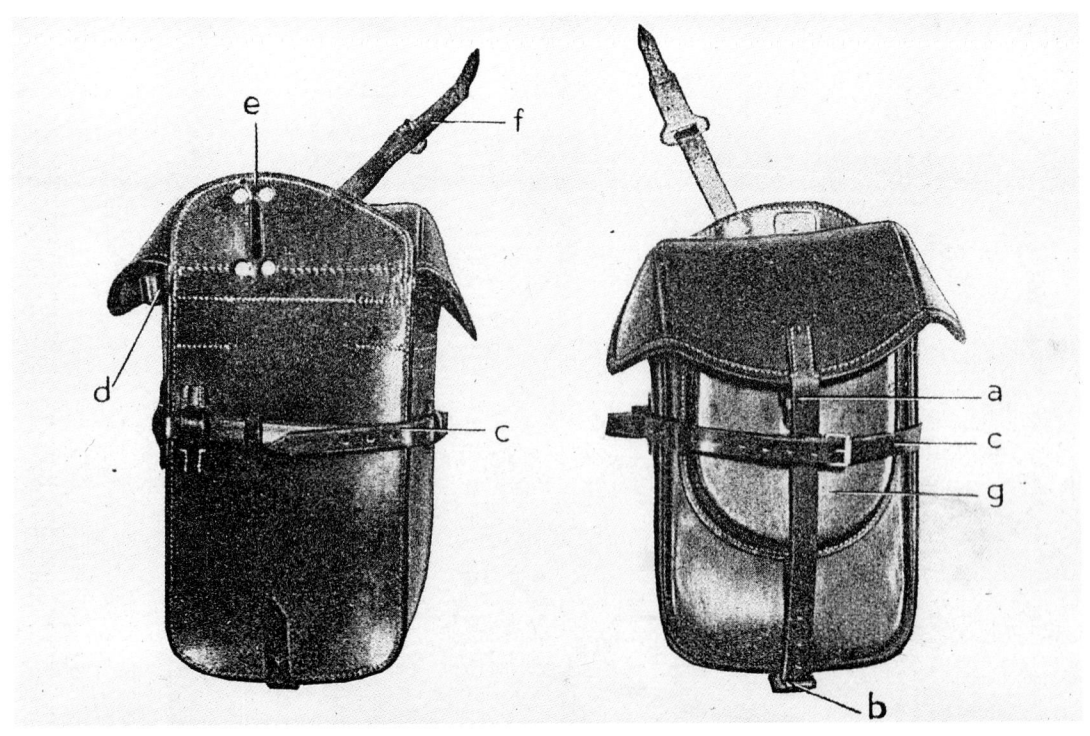

An example of pack arrangement in wartime.

Below: While on the march the horse-mounted troops had to keep the roads open for motorized troops. Horse troop of the 186th Reconnaissance Battalion in France, 1940.

The horse platoon of the 34th Infantry Regiment during the Western Campaign 1940. The troopers have taken advantage of a rest stop to feed the horses using the cloth water bags.

Whenever possible, troopers used larger metal containers to water their horses. Such containers had to be obtained from the train or taken from the land.

The 34th Reconnaissance Battalion's horse troop assembles following a patrol toward Condé sur Marne in France, 1940. A swastika flag had been draped over the horse on the extreme right; it was intended to serve as an air-identification panel.

Following the deletion of the rifle scabbard carrier at the end of 1940, horsemen generally carried their rifles slung across their backs. Horse troop of the 6th Reconnaissance Battalion in Russia, 1941.

The cavalry was capable of fording bodies of water; deeper bodies were crossed with, but also without, the assistance of the pioneers.

A horse troop cools the legs of its mounts during a rest stop. Note the new-style saddlebags behind the saddles, Russia 1941.

The great advantage of horse-mounted troops lay in their largely unrestricted mobility in nearly any terrain. The "star" on the upper left arm identifies its wearer as an Oberreiter (cavalry private, first class)

The 6th Horse Regiment (1st Cavalry Division) takes advantage of the opportunity to water its horses. A good view of the new-type saddlebags mounted behind the saddle and the front pack installed as a counterweight. Russia 1941.

kleine Packtasche

The new-style saddlebag (Packtasche neuer Art).

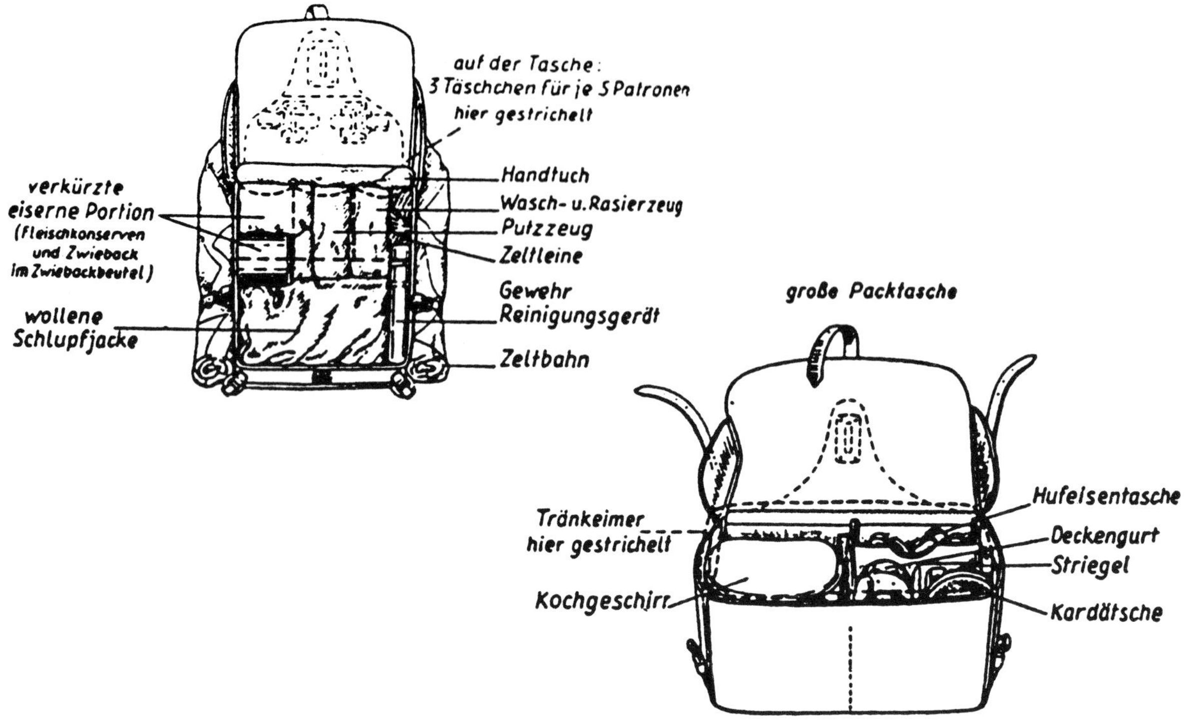

auf der Tasche:
3 Täschchen für je 5 Patronen
hier gestrichelt

verkürzte
eiserne Portion
(Fleischkonserven
und Zwieback
im Zwiebackbeutel)

Handtuch
Wasch- u. Rasierzeug
Putzzeug
Zeltleine
Gewehr
Reinigungsgerät

wollene
Schlupfjacke

Zeltbahn

große Packtasche

Hufeisentasche
Deckengurt
Striegel
Kardätsche

Tränkeimer
hier gestrichelt

Kochgeschirr

A typically armed and equipped cavalry section in Russia in 1941. The section leader carries an MPi 40, Type 35 message blank pouch and binoculars in carrying case. The troopers are armed with the Kar 98k. The Type 34 saddlebag was still used alongside the new-style saddlebag.

A horse troop's motorcycle dispatch rider in France 1940. Note the unit emblem on the fuel tank, a kettledrummer on horseback.

While a relatively light blanket of snow often posed problems even to vehicles equipped with snow-chains, it was no obstacle to the horse-mounted troops. Note the tactical symbol for the headquarters of a reconnaissance battalion on the left rear of the vehicle.

Horse artillery formed an indispensable part of the army cavalry. The 1st (East Prussian) Cavalry Brigade had a battalion of horse artillery, the 1st Cavalry Division later a regiment. The horse artillery differed from the horse-drawn artillery in that all gunners were horse-mounted. The horse artillery was seen as an elite group and was assigned specially-qualified officers and the best horses.

Unit	Officers	NCOs	Corporals	Enlisted Men	Horses	Horses Total
1st Horse Artillery Battalion						
HQ 1st Horse Btl.	9 + 1	19 + 1	15	10	14 R, 3 Re, 8 D	25
1st Battery, 1st Horse Btl.	6	30 + 1	33	77	77 R, 14 Re, 60 D	151
2nd Battery, 1st Horse Btl.	6	30 + 1	33	77	77 R, 14 Re, 60 D	151
3rd Battery, 1st Horse Btl.	6	30 + 1	33	77	77 R, 14 Re, 60 D	151
Bugler Corps, 1st Horse Btl.	1	21	3	3	29 R, 3 Re	32
Total:	28 + 1	130 + 4	117	244	274 R, 48 Re, 188 D	510

| | 524 soldiers | | | | | 510 horses |

Columns 2 and 3: + 1 = 1 medical officer or non-commissioned officer
Column 6: R = riding horse, Re = remount, D = draft horse

Tactical symbols of the horse artillery

 *Headquarters of a horse artillery battalion*

 Horse artillery field cannon

 Light artillery transport column

 Light artillery transport column (motorized)

 *Artillery march column*

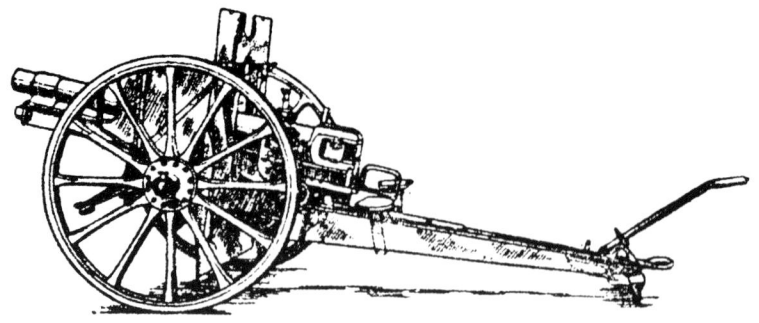

The classic weapon of the horse artillery was the lFK 16 light field cannon. Illustrated here is the redesigned version introduced in 1934; it had a rate of fire of 8-10 shots per minute.

Formed in 1939-40, the 1st Horse Artillery Regiment was equipped with the lFK 18 field cannon, which had been in production since 1938. At 1,120 kg, the new weapon was 400 kg lighter than the late version of the lFK 16 and had a split-trail gun carriage. Caliber was 75 mm, maximum firing range was given as 9,425 meters. Besides weighing less, its greatest advantage lay in its range of traverse of 60 degrees without need to move the trail. In the photo a lFH 18 of the 1st Horse Artillery Regiment during the fighting in Holland in 1940.

Bicycle troops, formation of which began in 1936, were intended to strengthen the infantry firepower of the cavalry regiments and in time of war reinforce the reconnaissance battalions. Light weapons and personal equipment could be carried on the standard army bicycle.

The light machine-gun team of a bicycle section with MG 34 and anti-aircraft tripod.

The shoulder straps of the officers and men of the 1st Bicycle Battalion bore a Gothic R.

1st machine-gunner with MG 34, which in wartime was attached to the crossbar of the army bicycle. Bicycle troop during the German entry into Paris 1940.

Each bicycle troop had a motorcycle section. Here B-Kräder (motorcycles with sidecar) of the IInd Battalion, 6th Cavalry Regiment, still without tactical insignia, during a parade in 1939.

The bicycle troop's heavy weapons, the heavy machine-gun and 50-mm mortar, were transported by motorcycle-sidecar combinations. Here a MG 34 with double drum magazine.

The bicycle troop was partially motorized. Apart from the three bicycle platoons, all elements of the troop were equipped with motorcycles or motor vehicles capable of cross-country travel. The troop's vehicle complement was thus 21 motorcycles, 17 with sidecar, and 7 all-terrain cars and trucks. Motorcyclists of the 6th Reconnaissance Battalion during the Western Campaign in 1940.

Bicycle platoons were capable of negotiating difficult terrain while retaining their mobility. A bicycle troop crosses a still-incomplete floating bridge. Western Campaign 1940.

Carriage of equipment during the war in the west in 1940. By the second year of the war army issue bicycles were already suffering badly from wear; however it proved possible to replace them with bicycles purchased in Holland, Belgium and France. The bicycle on the left of the photo (with white-painted fender), for example, was obtained that way.

Bicycle troop in Russia 1941. In contrast to Western Europe, where road conditions were good, in Russia the employment of bicycle units posed problems right from the outset. With the onset of the muddy period their use became practically impossible.

The SS Cavalry Divison also had a bicycle reconnaissance battalion, which in the beginning was organized and equipped like the army's 1st Bicycle Battalion. Stick hand grenades were sometimes carried stuck in the belt in the fashion of the infantry.

The Waffen-SS cavalry was equipped with modern camouflage uniforms in 1942. From the Bicycle Reconnaissance Battalion later emerged the Armored Reconnaissance Battalion of the 8th SS Cavalry Division Florian Geyer.

The bicycle troops of the Waffen-SS were also equipped with 50-mm mortars as heavy weapons; the mortar was referred to as "the poor man's artillery."

The 1st Cavalry Division, too, was partly motorized and its vehicle complement included a rather large proportion of motorcycles. Seen here is a motorcycle-sidecar bearing the division's unit emblem.

A bicycle troop of the 6th Cavalry Regiment returning to its home garrison (Bensheim) following the western campaign 1940. The troop commander's Kübelwagen displays the tactical symbol for a reconnaissance battalion.

THE CAVALRY GUN PLATOONS

Cavalry guns, first included in the Reichsheer budget in 1931 and then still designated as "mine projectors" for reasons of secrecy, continued to be used by the Wehrmacht. They were originally pulled behind a limber by a team of six horses, but in the cavalry regiments motor vehicles later replaced the horses. As well, the spoked wheels of the horse-drawn guns were replaced by metal wheels with rubber tires. A gun crew consisted of the gun commander and six gunners.

Below: Formed in 1939-40, the first cavalry regiments of the Waffen-SS were also equipped with the lIG 18. Note the leather insert of the breeches worn by the platoon commander (right side of photo).

Each platoon consisted of two guns (caliber 75 mm), which were capable of extremely accurate flat-trajectory and high-angle fire. This weapon was very popular with the field forces on account of its accuracy. This photo was taken in peacetime.

Below: In contrast to the army cavalry, the SS Cavalry Division continued to use the lIG 18, in its later form for use with motor vehicles, in the second half of the war as a light but effective weapon.

The gun crews were equipped like infantrymen. Before opening fire the trail spade had to be dug in; furthermore, the box-trail gun carriage had to be pushed down until it was seated by firing.

In the horse regiments the cavalry guns remained horse-drawn for the most part, as did those of non-motorized infantry divisions. On account of their small size and not very modern appearance, they were dubbed "gypsy artillery" by the field forces. The 1st Cavalry Brigade in Poland 1939.

The cavalry gun platoons of the horse regiments were also motorized before the start of the campaign against Russia. The G on the rear of the vehicle denoted Panzergruppe 2 (Guderian); beside it the "leaping horseman," the unit emblem of the 1st Cavalry Division. Photograph taken in Russia 1941.

One of the greatest advantages of the lIG 18 was its relatively light weight. This made it possible for the gun's crew to follow right behind the infantry or horse-mounted infantry while moving the weapon by hand.

One of the most potent additions to the cavalry in the final years of the Reichsheer resulted from the formation of anti-tank platoons, which at first were equipped with simulated weapons. Beginning in 1934 the
platoons were issued real 37-mm anti-tank guns and were motorized.

Below: The anti-tank platoon consisted of command, communications and ammunition vehicles as well as
three guns. These 37-mm Pak (anti-tank guns) wear standard Reichsheer camouflage colors, while the
vehicles still bear Reichswehr license plates; however, the men are wearing the national emblem of the
Wehrmacht. This photograph was probably taken in late 1934 or early 1935.

The vehicle most commonly used to tow the 37-mm anti-tank gun was the Kfz 69, the so-called "Krupp-Protze." The vehicle in the photo has had its windshield covered with a tarpaulin.

Below: The Krupp-Protze was fully capable of off-road travel and could transport the gun crew and the weapon's ammunition supply. Extremely popular with the troops, the vehicle remained in production until 1942.

The crew of the 37-mm anti-tank gun consisted of the gun commander and three men. This weapon could also be moved by hand on the battlefield through the use of towing belts.

Like the light infantry gun, the split-trail carriage of the 37-mm Pak had to be dug in before the first shot was fired and the trails
pressed down. To the right of the spade is an ammunition carrying case.

THE ARMORED RECONNAISSANCE PLATOONS

At the beginning of the 1930s the Reichsheer introduced lightly-armored reconnaissance vehicles, which were initially used by the motor transport units. In 1935 the cavalry, too, received such vehicles. They were the Kfz 13 and 14, both based on the Adler Standard 6 chassis. The two types were built as medium armored cars and were designated "machine-gun motor vehicle" and "radio motor vehicle" respectively. In the foreground of the photo is a machine-gun car, followed by a radio car, identifiable by its folding frame antenna. The white crosses on the vehicles suggest that the photo was taken during the campaign against Poland in 1939.

Below: In 1936 each Wehrmacht cavalry regiment formed an armored scout car platoon which consisted of three reconnaissance sections each with two Kfz 13 and a Kfz 14. The horse regiments received one armored scout car section. Here two armored cars of the 15th Cavalry Regiment's 10th (Heavy) Troop.

The Kfz 13 was not fully developed technically, possessed a limited ground clearance and offered its crew no armor protection above. For this reason, and because of its shape, it was dubbed "bathtub" by the troops. Although production of the Kfz 13 ceased in 1934, examples of the vehicle were still to be seen in service in the third year of the war. This Kfz 13 was photographed in 1941 during the Yugoslavian Campaign. A machine-gun car of the (former) 9th Cavalry Regiment, Fürstenwalde, it proved unable to negotiate the Balkan ravines.

Below: Beginning in 1939 the cavalry was assigned SdKfz 221 and 223 for use as armored reconnaissance cars, albeit in very limited numbers. Consequently only a few armored reconnaissance sections could be equipped with the new vehicles.

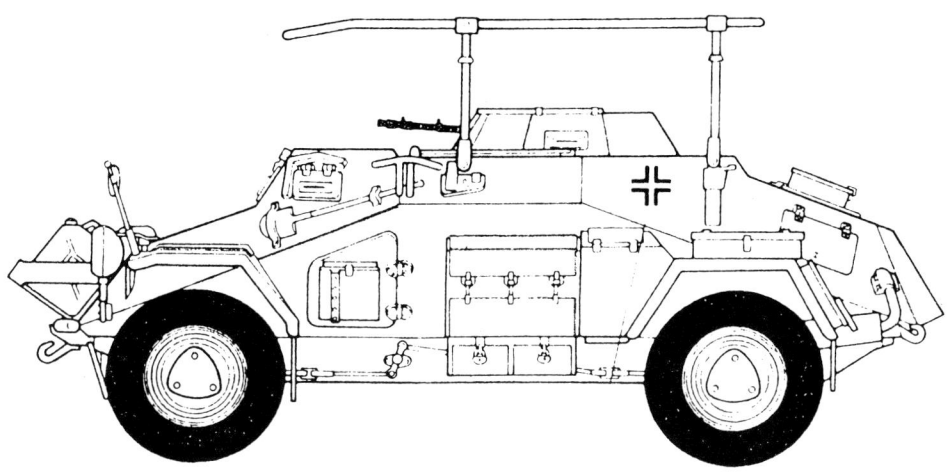

The technically improved Sonderkraftfahrzeug 221 possessed a more favorable shape than the Kfz 13 and was equipped with a rotating turret in which was mounted a MG 34 machine-gun. The SdKfz 223 radio car was equipped with a folding frame antenna.

The 6th Cavalry Regiment, for example, was issued SdKfz 223 radio cars but had to retain its Kfz 13 armored scout cars. The cavalry later ceased wearing the black (panzer) field uniform.

The cavalry's signal platoons were originally equipped with field telephone and signals equipment wagons. This mode of transport was retained only by the horse regiments within the 1st Cavalry Brigade, later Division.

The signals personnel of horse-mounted units laid field telephone lines by horse. Apart from their telephone equipment, in action the members of the field telephone sections were equipped the same as the riflemen of the cavalry section.

Below: The laying of field cable by horse was no simple matter; it called for a considerable degree of practice and skill.

Horse-mounted radio teams were equipped with the Tornisterfunkgerät b backpack radio set. They could be added to cavalry patrols and maintained contact with troop or battalion radio stations by means of cw transmission.

The Tornisterfunkgerät b installed in a service vehicle belonging to the motorized section of the 13th Cavalry Regiment's signals troop.

In 1940 signals platoons were formed for both Waffen-SS cavalry regiments; initially the army provided trained radio and telephone operators. Radio-communication exercise by the signals platoon of the 1st SS Cavalry Regiment in spring 1941 in Poland.

The backpack radio loaded on a pack horse.

With the formation of motorized platoons and troops in 1936, the signals platoons of cavalry and horse regiments were also partly motorized. A motorized field telephone section of the 1st Horse Regiment's signals platoon; the vehicles are Kfz 12, Stoever M 12.

In many instances the motorized field telephone sections used the Kfz 15, whose standard type was the Horch 830. In some cases this well-proven vehicle, which was built from 1933 to 1938, remained in service during the second half of the war.

The expansion of the army made it necessary to also place standard commercial vehicles into service. Vehicles of the signals troop of the 13th Cavalry Regiment during a parade held in Lüneburg on April 20, 1939. Note the tactical emblem of the 11th Troop, 13th Cavalry Regiment (partially-motorized) on the left fenders of the vehicles in the foreground.

Below: The motorized section of the signals platoon of a cavalry regiment of the 8th SS Cavalry Division in 1942. Note the unit emblem and tactical symbol on the fenders of the nearest vehicle.

A signals platoon of the 1st (East Prussian) Cavalry Brigade during the campaign in Poland 1939. A six-horse team made it possible to master even difficult road conditions.

Below: The signals platoon of the 2nd Horse Regiment during the advance into Russia 1941. In the east a six-horse team was indispensable, even for the relatively light signals vehicles.

Motorized radio section of the 13th Cavalry Regiment's signals troop in 1939. The radio section leader still wears the "cavalry helmet," the Oberreiter behind him the Stahlhelm M 18 steel helmet, and the two troopers on the right of the photograph the Stahlhelm 35. All the members of the section are wearing the little-loved "buckled boots." These were introduced between 1933 and 1935, after which production ceased. The vehicle bears no tactical symbol.

Below: Motorized signals platoon of the 13th Cavalry Regiment with four motor vehicles of different types. Lüneburg 1938.

CROSSING BODIES OF WATER

The cavalry was supposed to be capable of crossing bodies of water quickly, even without the assistance of the pioneers. Accordingly each horse or cavalry regiment was required to conduct at least one large-scale crossing exercise per year. Here troopers cross a river using self-procured means. Several of the troopers still wear the Reichsheer garrison cap. In the center of the photo is the troop bugler, identifiable by his "swallow's nests."

Below:
As a rule, large and small pneumatic floats were available for the crossing. Illustrated here is a large pneumatic float; the troopers wear the Reichsheer garrison cap.

Four swimming horses propelled each pneumatic float to the other side. This float exhibits Reichsheer camouflage colors.

Pneumatic float with drivers and draft horses of the horse-drawn vehicles. The horses are bridled on double-ring snaffles.

Deutsche Reiterhefte

Aufn. PK. Wiesenthal-Presse-Bild-Zentrale

HEFT 21 · 6. JAHRGANG · BERLIN, 10. OKTOBER 1941

Soldiers carry a small pneumatic float to the water. Three meters long, it could accommodate three men with their equipment.

While horse and rider could also cross bodies of water by swimming, taking their equipment and saddle kit with them in a "tent square bundle," bicyclists and motorized elements were always directed to use one of the various modes of water transport. River crossing by a motorcycle-sidecar of a bicycle troop.

Pneumatic floats were also used to erect temporary bridges, which accelerated river crossings considerably.

Below: June 22, 1941. A large field kitchen belonging to a reconnaissance battalion's horse troop crosses the River Bug.

The cavalry of the Wehrmacht had outstanding horse material at its disposal. No other army in the world chose, trained, cared for and fed its horses with such care as was traditional in the German Army. Consequently, its horses remained fit for service longer than in many other armies.

Similar care was given to the training of riders in peacetime by the cavalry and, with certain limitations, the artillery. Even though the Wehrmacht could not retain the original training period of 3,000 hours per rider on account of the relatively short compulsory service period, the training provided riders by the two branches of the service left nothing to be desired with regard to competence and thoroughness.

The training of riding and draft horses and all other horse-mounted and horse-drawn troops took part for the most part at the Military Area Riding and Driving Schools; consequently, in principle nearly all remount training in the Wehrmacht was undertaken by the cavalry. Training of young remounts at the Military Area Riding and Driving School at Dillingen, Danube.

Remounts were purchased at the age of three years by committees set up especially for that purpose. They subsequently spent one year in a remount office where, while doing no actual work, they were brought to a uniform standard of feeding and grooming. Training began at the age of four and encompassed another two years. Only the best riders in the troop were used in the first year (young remounts) and no serious demands were placed on the horses. Not until the second year of training (old remounts) were the young army horses introduced to the demands of actual military service.

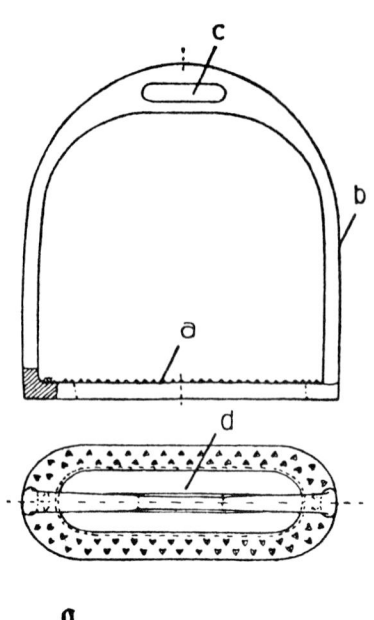

Stirrup
The stirrup is made of cast steel. It consists of the non-slip sole (a) and the stirrup body (b), in which is located the eye (c) for the stirrup strap. The sole is provided with a cutout (d).

Stirrup Strap
The stirrup straps (in three sizes) are equipped at one end with a double buckle with tongue (a) and no keeper, and at the other, pointed end with 16 buckle holes. The double buckle is pinned by straps of transparent leather. The stirrup straps are worn with the flesh side of the leather facing out.

Even after two years as a remount, training of army horses was continued by the units, with special emphasis being placed on dressage. Riding instructor of the 5th Cavalry Regiment on a talented and well-trained mount; it is bridled with a curb bit with a straight bar, which was less common in the army.

RI	=	*riding horse for officers*
KR	=	*riding horse for cavalry and infantry horse platoonss*
sZW	=	*heavy draft horse for the artillery*
sZK	=	*heavy draft horse for the other branches of the service*
ssZ	=	*heavy draft horse (heavy horse)*
R	=	*riding horse for other branches of the service*
ZI	=	*artillery wheel team*
Z	=	*swing team, lead, machine-gun horse*

Classification of army horses as of 1936; designations correspond to their various roles or branches of the service.

Two very typical "riding horses for officers" (RI) of the 2nd Horse Regiment, Angerburg, East Prussia. Rather average in size, they display a noble bearing and correct, straight legs. Their overall appearance suggests that they are of above average quality.

Newly-purchased horses of the ssZ class (heaviest draft horses). The Reichsheer did not use heavy draft horses. However, as loads to be transported became ever heavier after the advent of the Wehrmacht, and as the domestic supply of smaller horses was no longer sufficient to meet the demand for remounts, beginning in the mid-1930s the army also began purchasing heavy draft horses. During the war the cavalry, too, was assigned small numbers of heavy draft horses for use with horse-drawn vehicles.

Horse stable of the 6th Cavalry Regiment, Schwedt/Oder, 1936. Saddle and bridle were covered with the saddle blanket.

Bottom of facing page: Horse inspection. The veterinary officer inspects a service horse.

Below: Riding horse of a North-African Spahi Regiment captured in the campaign against France. Following the French Army's surrender the Wehrmacht took charge of large numbers of berber horses such as this one. As of 1943 they were assigned to the reorganized army cavalry.

KR-class horses of the 11th Horse Regiment, Neustadt, Upper Silesia. In 1934 this regiment became one of the first to be motorized; it was reorganized into 1st, 2nd and 3rd Motorcycle Battalions.

Horses ill-suited for use as mounts were usually employed as pack horses by the machine-gun or signals platoons.

Pack Saddle 33

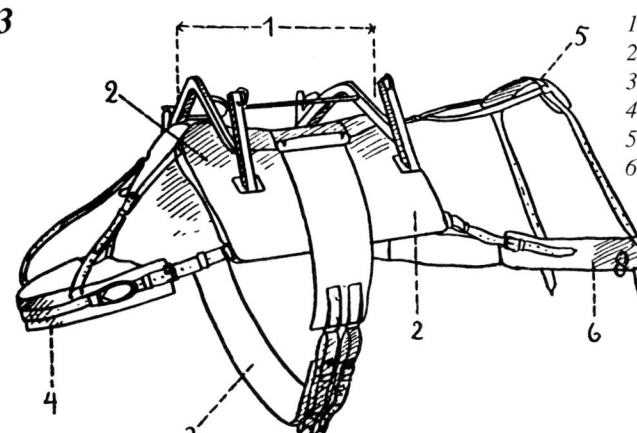

1. Pack saddle frame
2. Saddle pad
3. Girth
4. Martingale
5. Breeching
6. Breeching

Pack Saddle Frame

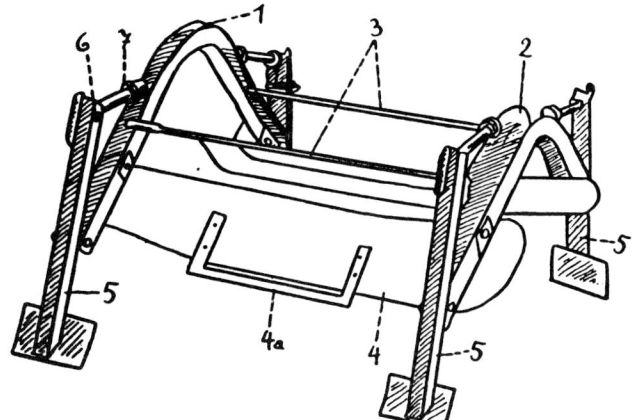

1. Front arch
2. Rear arch
3. Connecting rods
4. Saddle cover
4a. Loops for tightening girth
5. Frame rib
6. Adjusting bolt
7. Adjusting nut

Pack horse with the Packsattel 33 pack saddle and riding horse with Packtasche 34 saddlebags. The pack saddle frame as well as the "breeching" are clearly visible on the pack saddle.

143

The arrangement of the horse pack was changed often during the course of a campaign. This white horse, for example, carries an extensive front pack; these were avoided in peacetime in order to avoid placing pressure on the withers. The rider of the bay (below) has strapped another piece of baggage between the two saddle-bags.

The strand girth. Unlike the web girth, it consisted of eight broad strands held together by three leather keepers. Existing stocks were supposed to be "used up"; however, it remained in use during the war alongside the web girth.

Stable for draft horses which were driven from the saddle. The saddles have web girths, and the bridles the double-ring bit, which was often used with draft horses in place of a curb bit.

The Woilach, a coarse blanket, was generally used a saddle underpad. The saddle is equipped with a martingale and web girth. The rider is an Obergefreiter (corporal) and officer candidate of the 5th Cavalry Regiment, Stolp, Pomerania.

The riding horse's field equipment included the rear saddle pack, which consisted of the forage bag, over which was strapped the greatcoat or tent square.

These troopers are still equipped with the leather case for mess kit, which was attached to the right side of the saddle behind the rider (1936). Together with the forage bag, the mess kit case was later deleted in the course of a program to lighten the baggage carried by the cavalry.

Below: By 1938 the cavalry had already largely been motorized, outwardly recognizable by the Stahlhelm 35 helmet, which was predominantly worn, and the battledress tunic. Horse troop of the 13th Cavalry Regiment on the march to a battle maneuver. The helmet bands identify them as the "red" force. The Wachtmeister in the front wears the badge of a flag and standard bearer.

Motor vehicles were often preferred over trains for rapid relocations of cavalry units involving distances of between 60 and 200 kilometers. The horse-mounted section of a reconnaissance battalion's signals platoon during the entry into the Sudetenland in 1938.

Saddle horse equipment of the Waffen-SS cavalry at the start of the war. Type 34 saddlebags in front, and a sturdy, larger rear pack. Canteen on left side of saddle behind the rider.

*Troopers of the 15th Cavalry Regiment,
Paderborn, receiving their issue of hay
during a maneuver. The hay ration was
given out in the water bags, which were used
primarily as feed bags.*

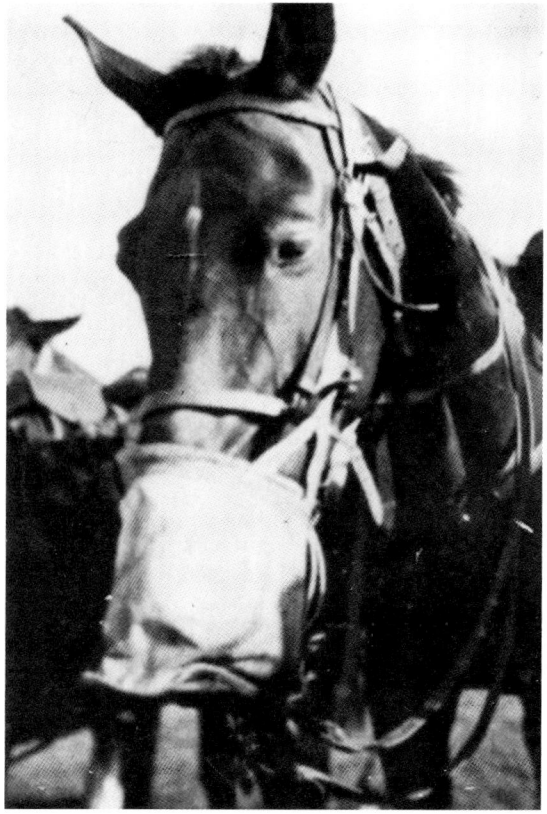

*An army horse takes feed from a water bag
which has been strapped over its nose.*

In the course of a baggage-lightening program, in 1941 a new type of forage bag was introduced which was carried in front of the horse's chest. Men and horses of the 2nd Horse Regiment in early 1941 during a maneuver in Poland.

A trooper during the fighting in Russia in 1942. A stick-type hand grenade is strapped to the left Type 34 saddlebag, the horse is bridled with a curb bit only and carries the new-style forage bag.

The cavalry's heavy weapons, as well as some of combat vehicles, were driven with six-horse teams to enable them to keep pace with the mounted riders.

Putting on the Sielengeschirr 25 breast harness.

Sielengeschirr 25 breast harness for driving from the saddle. The team consisted of wheelhorses, a swing team and lead horses.

Horse-drawn ammunition and weapons vehicles and pack horses were an indispensable part of cavalry operations.

Breaking-in wagon of the Military Area Riding and Driving School at Dillingen/Danube in 1942. The horses arrived at this training establishment at the age of four. There they were trained to the point where they could be employed by the field forces as young remounts.

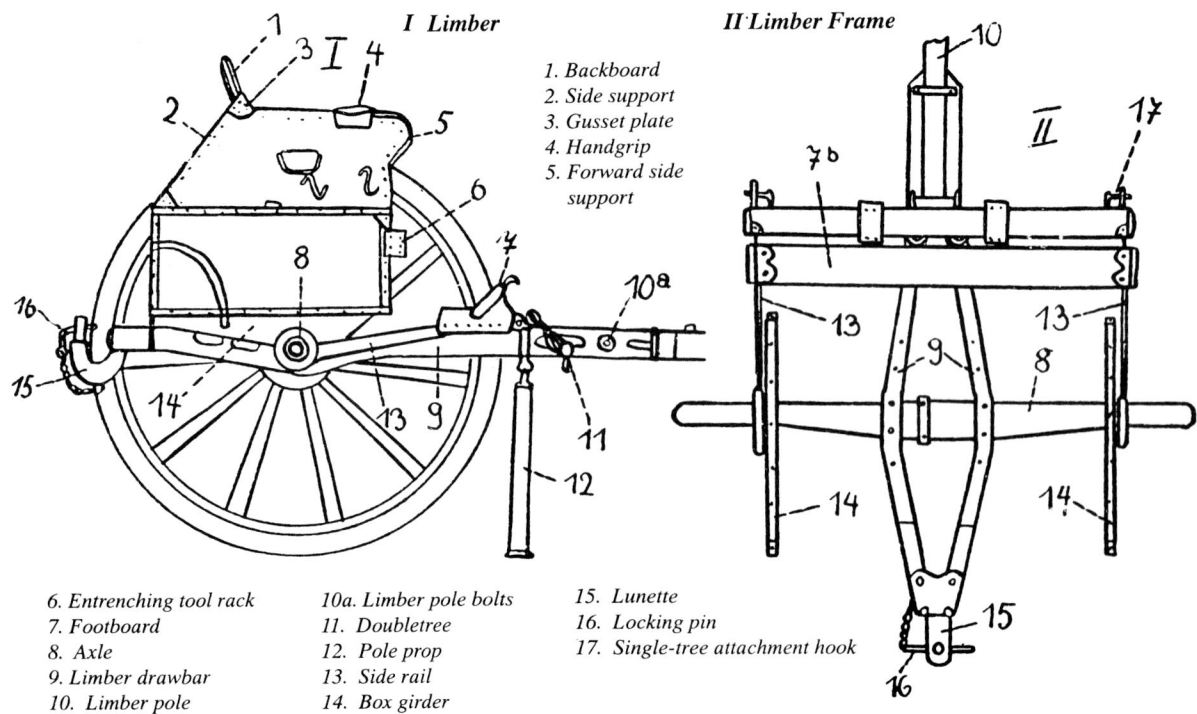

After driving in, the horses were familiarized with the different types of ammunition and weapons vehicle, here an Hf 1, as well as various terrain conditions.

Below: The limber was indispensable as a front wagon for every single-axle combat vehicle, with the exception of the infantry ammunition and weapons cart.

I Limber

1. Backboard
2. Side support
3. Gusset plate
4. Handgrip
5. Forward side support

II Limber Frame

6. Entrenching tool rack
7. Footboard
8. Axle
9. Limber drawbar
10. Limber pole

10a. Limber pole bolts
11. Doubletree
12. Pole prop
13. Side rail
14. Box girder

15. Lunette
16. Locking pin
17. Single-tree attachment hook

The train of every horse troop included a field kitchen, which was driven behind a limber.

Rear of a large field kitchen, 15th Cavalry Regiment, Paderborn.

Field kitchen with the train of a horse regiment of the 1st Cavalry Division in France, 1940.

Strapped onto the limber was a "large limber forage bag." It was 1.86 meters long, 75 centimeters wide and held 75 kilograms of oats.

In winter conditions the field kitchen could be separated from the axle and then temporarily mounted on a sleigh. SS Cavalry Brigade Fegelein, February 1942.

The Field Kitchen (Senking System) Trailer for use with motor vehicles. The cooker had a capacity of 250 liters. Field kitchens of this type were used by bicycle and heavy (motorized) troops.

The train of each horse troop also included a large blacksmith wagon, in the beginning an Hf 12. As of 1939 the Hf 7 steel field wagon was also employed for this purpose. Horseshoers of the 2nd Horse Regiment at work, Holland 1940.

Below: Two-horse team in front of an Hf 1 light field wagon, the most common ammunition and weapons vehicle used by horse-mounted and horse-drawn units. Type 25 breast harness for driving from the wagon-driver's seat. 5th Cavalry Regiment, Stolp.

The Hf 1 light field wagon. The vehicle weighed 610 kilograms empty and had a carrying capacity of 750 kilograms.

Hf 1 belonging to a troop of the 21st Horse Regiment, 1st Cavalry Division during the campaign in Russia, 1941.

It was standard practice, and good sense, to carry a spare wheel on the Hf 1 and Hf 2 ammunition and weapons wagons. France 1940.

Below: The Hf 2 heavy field wagon weighed 800 kilograms and could carry a load of 1,200 kilograms. Such a load required a team of at least four horses, usually of the ssZ class (heavy draft horses).

Even with a four-horse team it was no simple task for the horses and drivers of the Hf 2 to negotiate difficult terrain.

The wagon-driver's seat of an Hf 2. On the sideboard is the emblem of the 1st Cavalry Division. The spurs worn by the soldier on the right in fact identify him as a saddle driver. Russia 1941.

The Hf 2 heavy field wagon was ill-suited for use by the cavalry troops on account of its heavy loaded weight. Instead it was more commonly used by supply transport columns and horse-drawn units.

Below: Much of the train, but also the vehicles of the transport columns and supply units, were not with the field units during peacetime. Only when mobilization was ordered were they taken into the service of the Wehrmacht. Most were agricultural or commercial vehicles. Light transport column with agricultural vehicles, 1940.

A large number of steel field wagons with rubber tires were issued to horse-mounted and horse-drawn units shortly before the outbreak of the Second World War. This left the troops insufficient time to become familiar with this new type of vehicle before taking it into action.

The steel field wagon, whose official designation was "Large Field Wagon Hf. 7/11," weighed 1,040 kilograms and possessed a carrying capacity of 1,720 kilograms. A four-horse team proved necessary in practice, which caused considerable difficulties in surmounting obstacles during the Western Campaign.

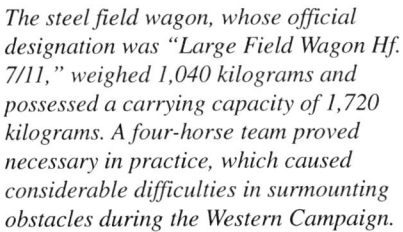

The design and weight of the army's ammunition and weapons vehicles made them poorly suited to the terrible road conditions in Russia; for this reason the troops equipped themselves with locally-used, light horse-drawn vehicles whenever possible.

A typical scene from the advance into Russia 1941. Horse-drawn vehicles share the road with motorized units, bicyclists and cavalry. In the foreground an Hf 1 light ammunition and weapons wagon with a two-horse team.

THE ARMY CAVALRY 1943-1945

After its reestablishment in 1943, the army cavalry was supposed to receive the new MG 42 machine-gun as standard equipment. In the end, however, this requirement proved impossible to meet.
From right to left: Generalfeldmarschall von Kluge, Major von Boeselager and Rittmeister von Boeselager inspecting weapons and equipment delivered to Cavalry Regiment Center.

This photo, taken during firing practice while Cavalry Regiment Center was in the formation phase, shows that the Karabiner 98k and the MG 34 were still the standard weapons of the cavalry troops. The Wachtmeister on the left side of the photo is armed with the P 08 pistol. The P 38 pistol was rarely encountered in the cavalry.

The pistol holsters of the P08 (left) and P 38.

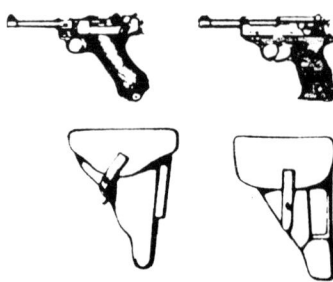

9-mm-Pistole Walther „P 38"

The new cavalry regiments were issued a number of Kettenkrad half-tracked vehicles to help ease the problem of supplying the horse-mounted units.

Vehicles of Cavalry Regiment Center's Ist Battalion on the road from Strygalov to Dolsk in the autumn of 1943.

Members of Cavalry Regiment Center photographed in the winter of 1943-44. The reborn, modern cavalry could not have gotten along without motor vehicles. Compared to 1941-42 the clothing situation had improved considerably. Like all combat troops, the cavalrymen were also equipped with the reversible camouflage uniform.

Right: For extreme weather conditions there was the winter suit, which came in three versions. Seen here is the winter jacket with attached hood and rank badge on the upper sleeve, as introduced on August 22, 1942. The rank badge identifies this officer as a Leutnant.

The scout platoons of the horse regiments were partly equipped with the VW Schwimmwagen, which had a very positive effect on their performance.

Schwimmwagen with camouflage tarpaulin lashed down in front of the windshield. 32nd Horse Regiment in the winter of 1944-45.

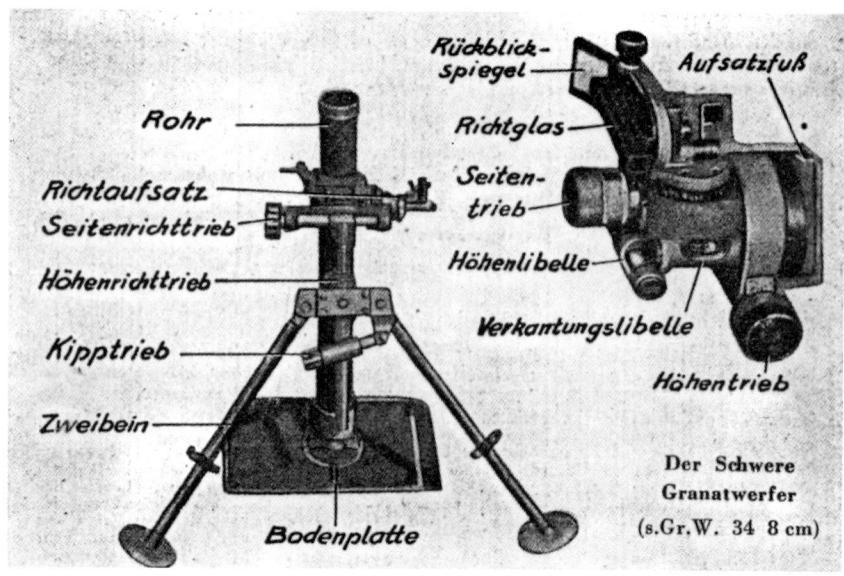

The heaviest weapon possessed by each horse battalion was the mortar troop, with twelve mortars (80-mm) and a strength of 231 men and 254 horses. Training on the sGrW 34 heavy mortar in Russia 1944.

The Type 34 heavy mortar.

Rückblick-
spiegel
Aufsatzfuß
Rohr
Richtglas
Richtaufsatz
Seiten-
trieb
Seitenrichttrieb
Höhenrichttrieb
Höhenlibelle
Kipptrieb
Verkantungslibelle
Zweibein
Höhentrieb
Bodenplatte
Der Schwere
Granatwerfer
(s.Gr.W. 34 8 cm)

Light, single-axle horse-drawn vehicles for transporting mortars were manufactured for the army. Drawn by a tandem team of horses, they were capable of negotiating even the narrowest path. Cavalry Regiment Center.

The horse troops received a considerable increase in firepower with the introduction of the MPi 43, which was later designated the Sturmgewehr (Assault Rifle) 44. Troops of the 5th Cavalry Regiment in Russia.

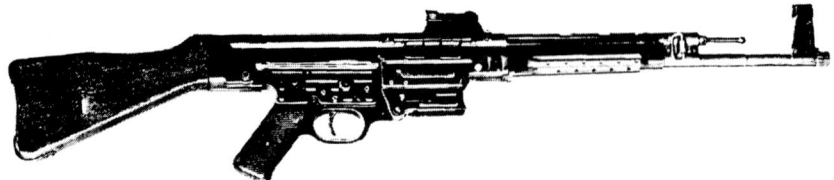

The 7.92-mm MP 43, MP 44 and StG 44.

The machine-gun troops remained largely equipped with the heavy version of the MG 34. The cavalry was not totally reequipped with the MG 42, probably on account of the general shortage of materiel that existed late in the war. A machine-gun troop of the 32nd Horse Regiment, Russia 1944.

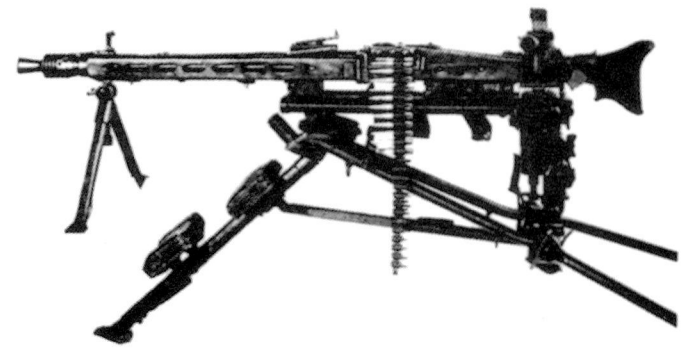

The MG 42 mounted on a tripod base for use as a heavy machine-gun.

Formed in 1944, the Ist Cavalry Corps had under its command the 3rd and 4th Cavalry Brigades and the 1st Hungarian Cavalry Division.

In terms of equipment and armament, the Hungarian cavalry division was ill-suited to the demands of the second half of the war. The equipment carried by the rider in the center of the photo is most interesting. Mounted on his saddle is a type of battle axe. Russia 1944.

Not until 1943 was a cavalry division formed from the numerous cossack formations serving as auxiliaries in the Wehrmacht. The cossacks wore their traditional fur hat, in some cases with the German national emblem, with the standard German battledress tunic.

A cossack uniform was introduced for special occasions; it closely resembled the uniforms worn during the time of the czars.

Despite being issued heavy weapons, cossack units were primarily security forces; they were, however, also used in an offensive role in anti-partisan warfare. The units of the 1st Cossack Cavalry Division had German cadre personnel, in some cases to the level of subordinate commander.

May 1945. The XVth Cossack Cavalry Corps surrenders in the part of Austria occupied by English forces; soon afterward, however, the latter handed the cossacks over to the Soviet Union.

By the year 1944 the cavalry of the Waffen-SS consisted of two complete divisions. In addition to three cavalry regiments and other units, each division included a large proportion of armored units – an armored reconnaissance battalion, an anti-tank battalion, an anti-aircraft battalion and an assault gun battalion. The latter emerged from the independent assault gun battery which had been a part of the SS Cavalry Division since 1942.

Here the battery's assault guns entrain in preparation for an action near Kharkov in August 1943.

Typical equipment carried by the Waffen-SS cavalry. The trooper on the right holds a so-called "driver's eel" under his arm, which identifies him as a saddle driver.

Dismounted Waffen-SS cavalrymen move up for an attack. The officer (second from the right) wears privately-bought riding boots with stiff shanks and privately-bought breeches.

Members of the 8th SS Medical Battalion (8th SS Cavalry Division) tending to wounded on the battlefield. The photo shows the spotted camouflage of the helmet cover and camouflage jacket as well as the carriage of the P 08 pistol.

A 20-mm anti-aircraft gun of the SS Cavalry Brigade on a makeshift winter carriage, during the fighting for Rzhev, a key point on the Eastern Front, in the winter of 1942.

The Assault Gun Battery, like the assault gun battalion of the 8th SS Cavalry Division which succeeded it, was equipped with the StuG III Ausf. F or G.

This vehicle was also designated the Sturmgeschütz 40. Its armament consisted of a 75-mm StuK L/43 or L/48 and a single machine-gun behind an armor shield. Tactically, attacks by assault guns with troopers riding on the vehicles were inadvisable, but following the dictates of the moment they were almost always the rule.

Beginning in 1942 the heavy troops of the Waffen-SS cavalry began receiving the 50-mm anti-tank gun, which was transported by the Maultier tracked truck. On the left side of the tailgate is the tactical symbol and on the right the unit emblem of the 8th SS Cavalry Division Florian Geyer.

The SS Cavalry Brigade, as well as the later divisions or elements of these, frequently served under the command or army corps or divisions, which resulted in a high degree of cooperation between the units. General von Sudnitz, the commanding officer of the 87th Infantry Division, decorates cavalry officers and troopers of the Waffen-SS.

Although camouflage clothing was standard in the Waffen-SS cavalry, in some cases the battledress tunic continued to be worn in action. Seen here is an SS-Hauptscharführer, the Spiess, or senior non-commissioned officer, of a cavalry troop.

In contrast to the Army's 3rd and 4th Cavalry Brigades, the cavalry divisions of the Waffen-SS continued to use the lIG 18 light infantry gun in their heavy troops. Here a Kfz 18 serves as a gun tractor. The emblem of the 8th SS Cavalry Division, a horse's head and sword, is plainly visible on the right rear of the vehicle.

An assault gun with extra-wide winter tracks, a combination rarely photographed. The vehicle belongs to the Assault Gun Battalion of the 8th SS Cavalry Division Florian Geyer. On June 28, 1944 the assault guns were incorporated into the division's anti-tank battalion.

These two photos illustrate quite clearly the difference between the spotted camouflage of the uniforms worn by the army and the Waffen-SS. On the left is Generalmajor Holste, commander of the 4th Cavalry Brigade . . .

. . . on the right SS-Obersturmführer Geier, troop commander in the SS Cavalry Brigade.

The camouflage uniform introduced by the Waffen-SS in 1942 served as the model in color and style for the camouflage clothing later adopted by many armies.

Troopers of the 17th SS Cavalry Regiment wearing the winter suit with parka, which provided complete winter camouflage. The 22nd SS Volunteer Cavalry Division Maria Theresia was created from this regiment in spring 1942.

"Cabling" (assigning of horses) of remounts by the 3rd Cavalry Brigade in August 1944 on the Eastern Front. While replacing losses in materiel became increasingly difficult during the final years of the war, the replacement of horses continued in a satisfactory manner until the end.

Cavalrymen of the 31st Horse Regiment of the 3rd Cavalry Brigade in Russia in 1944. In spite of partial mechanization, until 1945 the brigade – later division – had a complement of 11,000 horses, which was equal to approximately two-thirds the complement of the 1st Cavalry Division in 1941.

Officers and men of the 5th Cavalry Regiment Feldmarschall von Mackensen on the morning of May 11, 1945, the day the unit surrendered to English forces in Austria. The officer on the right side of the photo wears the division emblem on his upper right sleeve and the cuff title of the regiment on the lower sleeve.

Horse-mounted field telephone section during peacetime training.

TACTICAL SYMBOLS

Cavalry

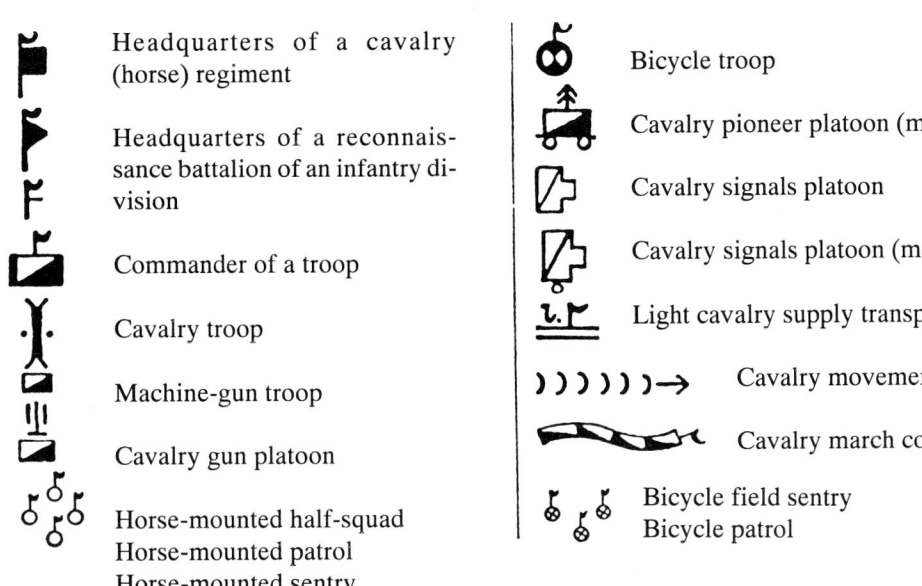

Headquarters of a cavalry (horse) regiment

Headquarters of a reconnaissance battalion of an infantry division

Commander of a troop

Cavalry troop

Machine-gun troop

Cavalry gun platoon

Horse-mounted half-squad
Horse-mounted patrol
Horse-mounted sentry

Bicycle troop

Cavalry pioneer platoon (motorized)

Cavalry signals platoon

Cavalry signals platoon (motorized)

Light cavalry supply transport column

Cavalry movements

Cavalry march column

Bicycle field sentry
Bicycle patrol

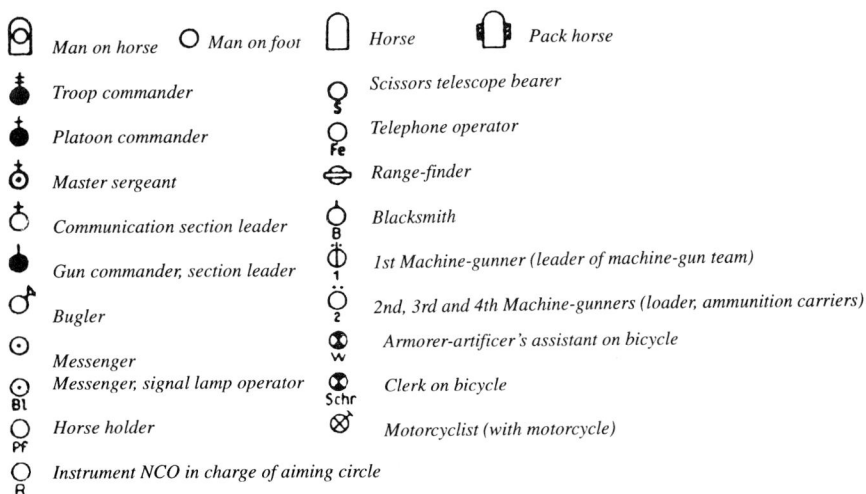

Man on horse   *Man on foot*   *Horse*   *Pack horse*

Troop commander   *Scissors telescope bearer*

Platoon commander   *Telephone operator*

Master sergeant   *Range-finder*

Communication section leader   *Blacksmith*

Gun commander, section leader   *1st Machine-gunner (leader of machine-gun team)*

Bugler   *2nd, 3rd and 4th Machine-gunners (loader, ammunition carriers)*

Messenger

Messenger, signal lamp operator   *Armorer-artificer's assistant on bicycle*

Horse holder   *Clerk on bicycle*

Instrument NCO in charge of aiming circle   *Motorcyclist (with motorcycle)*

Further Symbols Introduced in 1938

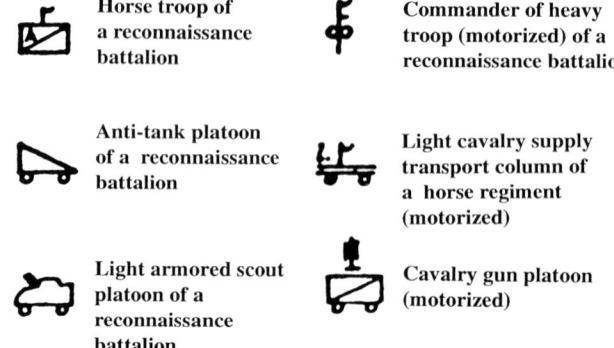

Horse troop of a reconnaissance battalion

Commander of heavy troop (motorized) of a reconnaissance battalion

Anti-tank platoon of a reconnaissance battalion

Light cavalry supply transport column of a horse regiment (motorized)

Light armored scout platoon of a reconnaissance battalion

Cavalry gun platoon (motorized)

The Karabiner 98b temporarily returned to service with some of the cavalry formations newly created at the start of the war. The officer seen here wears a pistol which he purchased privately. The troopers are part of the German occupation forces stationed on the Channel Coast of France.

Army Cavalry in The Second World War

Unit	Primary Composition		In Service
	(a) Cavalry	(b) Divisional Units	
1st (East Prussian) Cavalry Brigade	2 horse regiments 1 bicycle battalion	1 horse artillery battalion 1 pioneer company 1 supply company	1939
1st Cavalry Division	4 horse regiments 1 bicycle battalion	1 horse artillery regiment 1 signals battalion 1 pioneer battalion, 1 anti-tank company supply-administration services	1939-41
Cavalry Regiments Center, North and South	3 horse regiments	1 artillery battalion, 1 heavy battalion supply-administration services	1943-44
3rd Cavalry Brigade and 4th Cavalry Brigade (later divisions)	2 horse regiments 1 heavy cavalry battalion 1 replacement-training battalion	1 pioneer company supply-administration services	1944-45
SS Cavalry Brigade Fegelein	2 horse regiments 1 bicycle reconnaissance battalion	1 horse artillery battalion pioneer company, signals company flak battery supply-administration services	1941-42
8th SS Cavalry Division (later Florian Geyer)	3, later 4 cavalry regiments 1 bicycle reconnaissance battalion	armored reconnaissance battalion (added later) 1 anti-tank battalion 1 artillery regiment 1 flak battalion 1 signals battalion 1 pioneer battalion 1 assault gun battery, later battalion supply and medical units	1944-45
22nd SS Volunteer Cavalry Division Maria Theresia	organized like the 8th SS Cav.Div. with minor deviations		1944-45
37th SS Volunteer Cavalry Division Lützow	2 cavalry regiments	1 artillery battalion 1 pioneer battalion supply-administration services	1945
1st Cossack Cavalry Division	6 horse regiments later 3 horse regiments	2 artillery battalions 1 signals battalion 1 pioneer battalion administration-supply units	1943-45
2nd Cossack Cavalry Division	3 horse regiments	1 artillery battalion pioneer, signals, administration and supply units	1945

Cavalry Regiment Center 1943

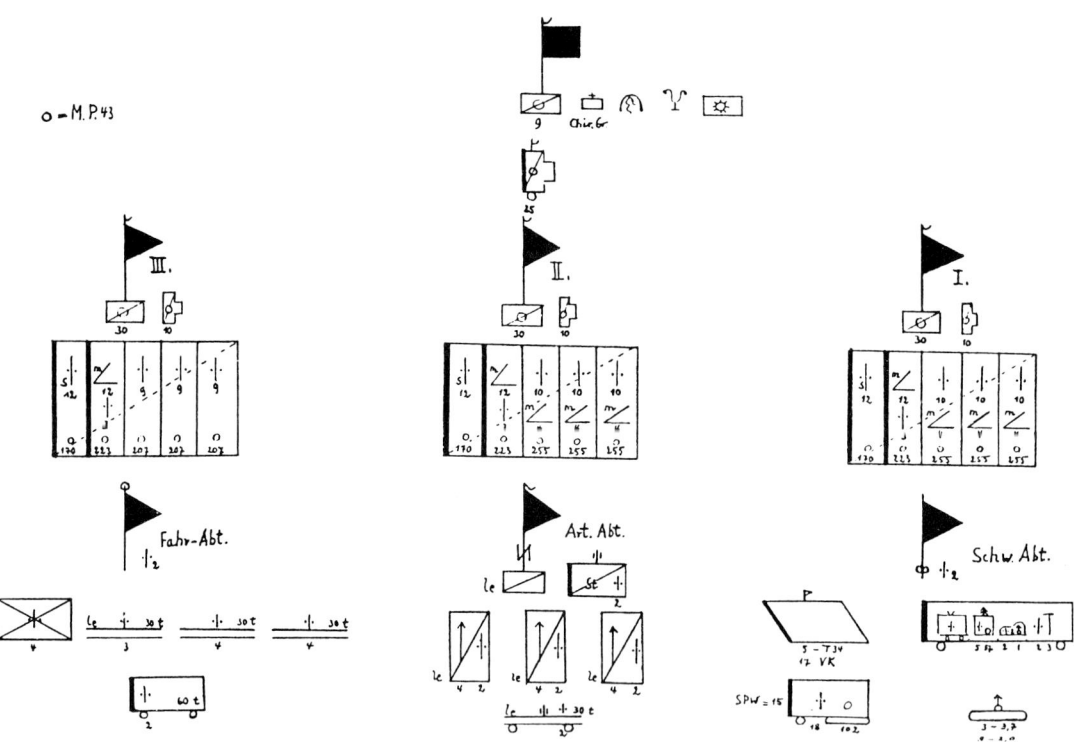

The SS Cavalry Division 1943

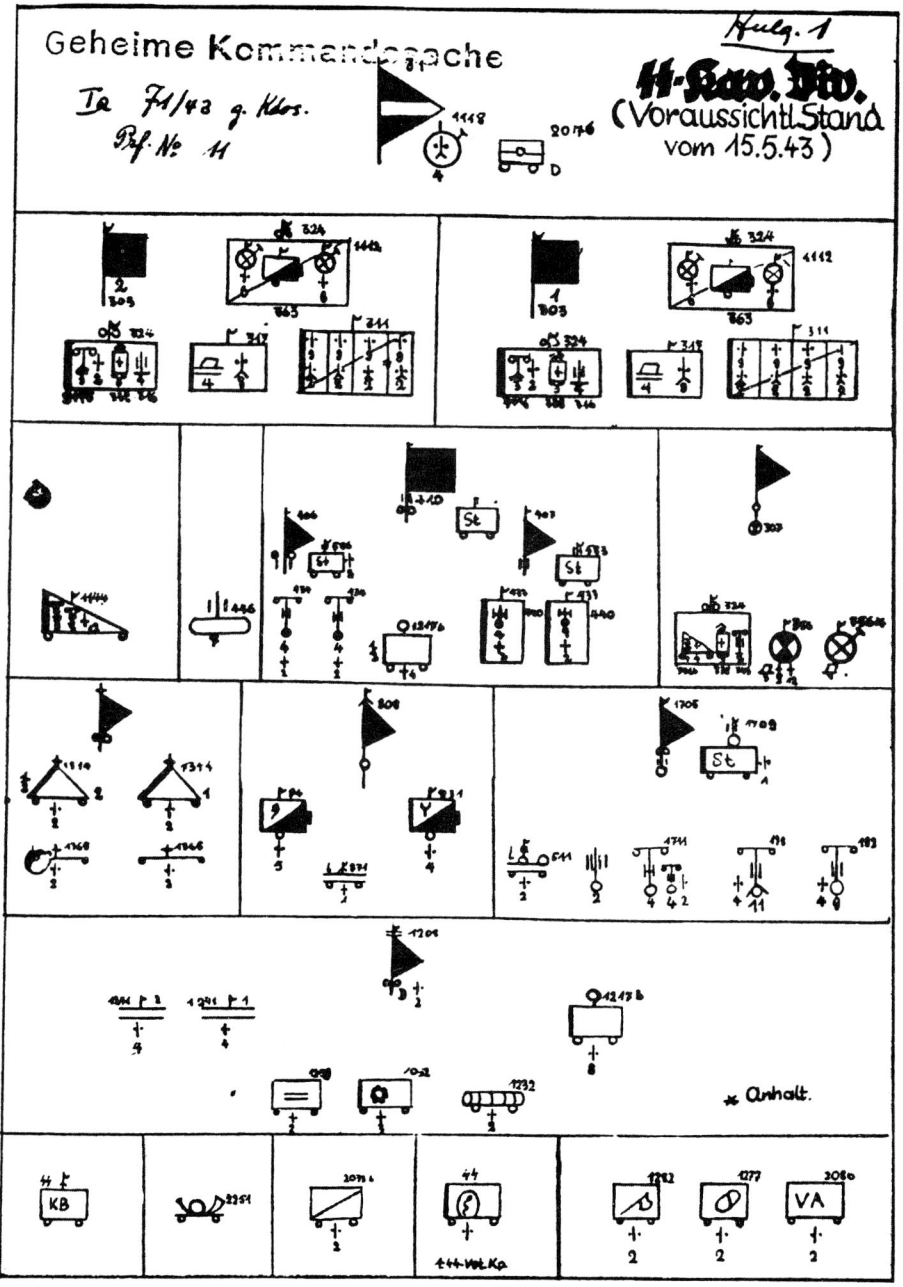

191

Strength and Equipment Return of a Horse Regiment 1944

Table of Organization (Army) Military Budget 44

Headquarters and Headquarters Troop of a Horse Regiment

	(a) HQ	(B) HQ	Troop Squad Leader	Signals Platoon	Scout Platoon	Pioneer Platoon	Anti-tank Platoon Train	Total
Officers	7	1	1	1	1	1	3	15
Officials	-	-	-	-	-	-	2	2
NCOs	1	5	16	3	5	4	19	53
Enlisted Men	18	4	65	32	42	28	73	262
Riding Horses	24	10	15	-	-	-	2	51
Draft Horses	-	-	12	-	-	-	20	32
Pack Animals	-	-	-	-	-	-	-	-
Carbines	9	3	65	4	15	25	68	189
Submachine-guns	17	3	17	25	29	5	2	98
Pistols		-	4	-	7	43	27	45
Machine guns	-	-	1	3	-	3	1	12
Guns	-	-	-	-	- 3 (75-mm Pak) -			3
Horse-drawn Vehicles	-	-	5	-	-	-	5	10
Motorcycles	3	-	-	2	1	1 -	7	
Cars	3	-	3	10	1	1	2	20
Trucks		-	11					
	-	5	1	20.	37			
RSO	-	-	-	-	-	3	-	3
Armored Vehicles	-	-	1	-	-	-	-	1

Headquarters and Headquarters Troop of a Horse Battalion

	(A) HQ	HQ Troop Squad Leader		Signals Platoon	Train	Total
Officers	6	1		1	"-	8
Officials		"-	"-	5	13	20
NCOs	2	"-		5	13	20
Enlisted Men	14	1		35	31	81
Riding Horses	16		"-	32	4	54
Draft Horses		"-	"-	10	28	38
Pack Animals		"-	"-	9	"-	9
Carbines		"-	"-	13	21	34
Submachine-guns	19	1		28	18	66
Pistols	6	1	"-		7	14
Machine-guns		"-	"-	"-	1	1
Horse-drawn Vehicles		"-	"-	2	7	9
Motorcycles	3	"-	"-		1	4
Motor Vehicles	3	"-	"-		8	11

	Horse Troop of a Horse Regiment	Mortar Troop of a Horse Regiment	Machine-gun Troop of a Horse Regiment
Officers	3	3	3
NCOs	35	32	39
Enlisted Men	186	152	189
Riding Horses	196	146	179
Draft Horses	34	60	76
Carbines	80	29	42
Assault Rifles	124	-	-
Sniper Rifles	6	-	-
Submachine-guns	-	127	179
Light Machine-guns	6	1	4
Heavy Machine-guns	-	12	-
Mortars	-	"-	12 (80-mm)
Horse-drawn Vehicles	9	21	30
Other Vehicles	1	2	2
Motorcycles	"-	2	2
Cars	1	3	4

Cavalry section with equipment in early 1941.

Organization of a Cavalry Brigade 1945

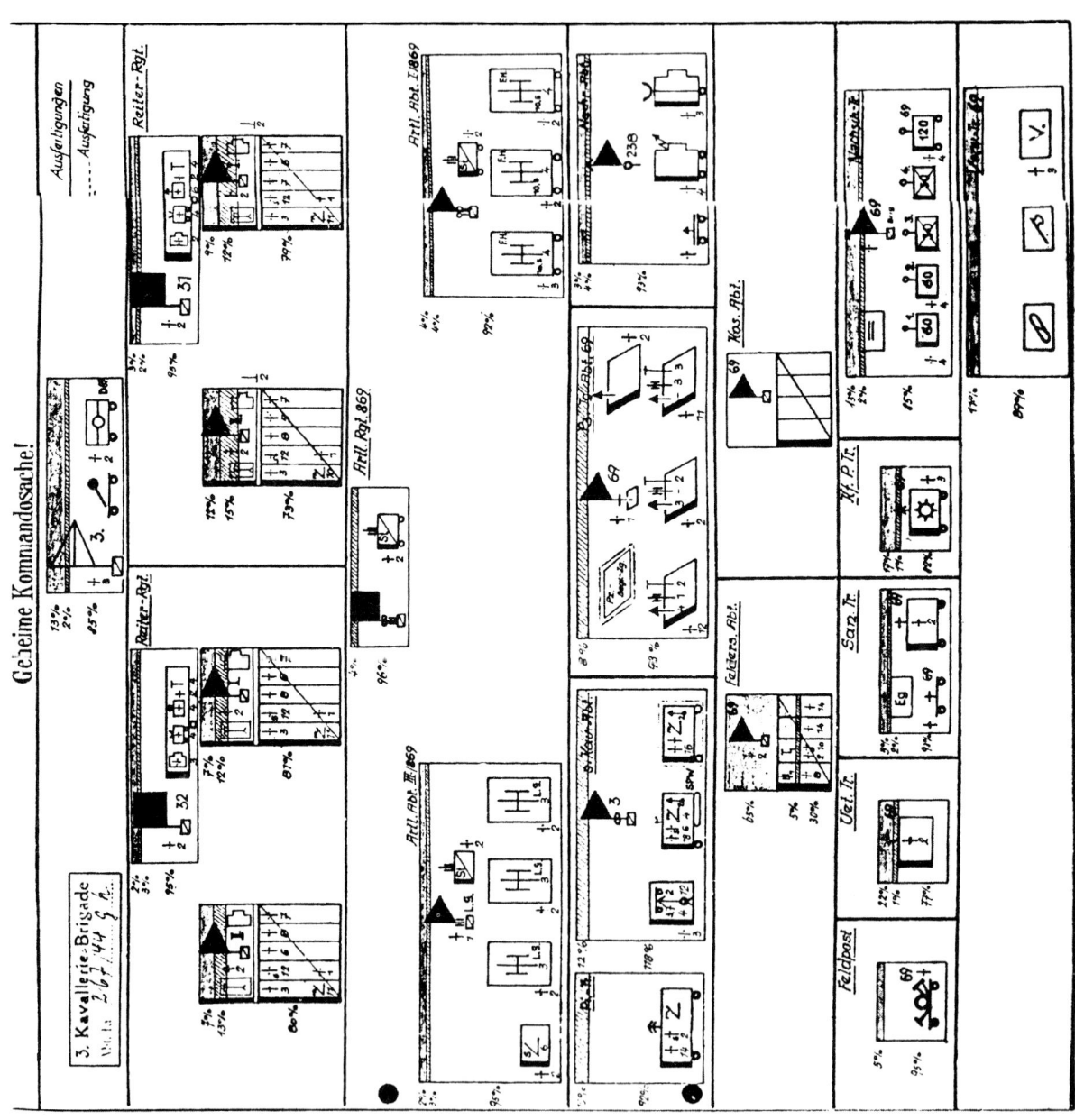

194

Unit Emblems

1st Cavalry Division (the Leaping Horseman) later the 24th Panzer Division

Cavalry Regiment Center

Cavalry Regiment South

**8th SS Cavalry Division
Florian Geyer**

**22nd SS Volunteer Cavalry Division
Maria Theresia**

**37th SS Volunteer Cavalry
Division
Lützow**

Sleeve Badges

Vth Cossack Cavalry Corps

The Cossack Regiment

Kuban Cossack Regiment

Terek Cossack Regiment

Siberian Cossack Regiment

4th Cavalry Division

Commemorative Badges

Worn on the peaked cap and garrison cap between the national eagle and cockade; also worn on the shoulder straps of offers and men of the 5th Cavalry Regiment.

Prussian Death's Head

of the Bodyguard Hussars Regiments No. 1 and No. 2, worn by the 1st and 2nd Troops, 5th Horse Regiment; later HQ, Bugle Corps and Ist Battalion, 5th Cavalry Regiment, minus the 3rd Troop (Blücher Hussars).

1943 taken over by Cavalry Regiment North, later renamed the 5th Cavalry Regiment Feldmarschall von Mackensen.

Brunswick Death's Head

in the cavalry worn by the 4th Troop, 13th Horse Regiment, later IInd Battalion, 13th Cavalry Regiment; 1943 taken over by Cavalry Regiment South, later the 41st Horse Regiment.

Dragoon Eagle

also called "Swedte Eagle," originally worn by the 1st Brandenburg Dragoon Regiment No. 2, adopted by the 2nd and 4th Troops of the 6th Horse Regiment, later 6th Cavalry Regiment.

Taken over by Cavalry Regiment Center in 1943 and then by the entire 3rd Cavalry Brigade in 1944.

Cuff Bands

**It was not possible to issue the cuff bands
to all front-line forces.**

SS Cavalry Division

**8th SS Cavalry Division Florian Geyer The
cavalry unit of the Waffen-SS, initially a brigade, was expanded into the SS Cavalry Division in 1942, and when all divisions of the
Waffen-SS were numbered in 1943 was assigned the number 8.**

Florian Geyer

**Florian Geyer
The division was awarded a new cuff band
when the name Florian Geyer was bestowed.**

Feldmarschall v. Mackensen

Feldmarschall von Mackensen

**The 5th Cavalry Regiment, which was declared a special unit in 1944, received the title
Feldmarschall von Mackensen on the 95th birthday of this First World War army commander.**

The Horseman's Badge

In the 1930's the "National Association for the Breeding and Testing of German Warm Bloods" (a breed of horse) introduced the horseman's badge in classes bronze, silver and gold. It was intended that it should serve as a stimulus to enhance the level of training in all areas of the riding field. Bronze and silver classes were awarded following the completion of a special test in which the applicant demonstrated the required degree of riding skill and theoretical knowledge of the anatomy, behavior and care of the horse. Since the army represented one of the largest rider training organizations in the country, officers with the rank of Rittmeister serving as troop commanders and those with the rank of Hauptmann in the horse-drawn or horse artillery serving as battery commanders were required to take both the military and civilian tests. Surprisingly the field forces made little or no use of them.

Part of the reason for this may lie in the fact that during the years of the reformation of the army the rigorous duty schedule left little time for the preparation and administering of the test. Another reason is that the cavalrymen and artillerymen looked upon their riding skills as part and parcel of their profession, which did not have to be made a show of by the wearing of a special badge. Most of the uniformed personnel who did wear the horseman's badge did not belong two the two named branches of the service.

Replacement and Supplemental Acquisition of Horses

The Wehrmacht was the largest owner of horses in the German Reich. In addition to a comparatively small number of carrier pigeons and messenger and first-aid dogs, in peacetime the army had at its disposal a complement of more than 180,000 horses, including several hundred mules.

Of that number the infantry accounted for approximately 50%, the artillery 36% and the cavalry 12%. The remaining 2% were used by the pioneer corps, the signals corps, the schools, senior staffs and other army installations. When mobilization was implemented in 1939, the field forces were assigned 15,000 horses by the remount offices; however, in order to reach the required wartime strength of 855,000 horses, a further 660,000 had to be conscripted in the old Reich under the provisions of the Reich War Measures Act. The latter contained a "Supplemental Acquisition of Horses Regulation" which described to the last detail how the acquisition of additional horses was to be carried out.

Extract from the Reich War Measures Act

III. Horses and Horse-drawn Vehicles

20. Supplemental Acquisition of Horses Regulation (PfdErgV)

Of 13 August 1938 (Armed Forces Gazette PP 567) with the Amendments of 23 December 1938 (Armed Forces Gazette PP 1042).

The following regulation for the supplemental acquisition of horses is issued according to Section 33 of the act concerning measures for defense purposes (war measures act) of 13 July 1938 (Reich Law Gazette I, PP 887).

Table of Contents

Running in parallel to the supplementary acquisition of horses was the so-called horse re-placement process, which was ongoing in times of peace and war. Three remount committees were responsible for the program in peacetime, six during wartime. They purchased replace-ment horses on the public and private markets; usually 3 to 4 years of age, the horses were designated "remounts." In peacetime the remounts usually spent one year in a remount office where they were brought to a uniform state of feeding and care. During the war, horses four years and older often had to be placed directly into training. As a rule the replacement horses were of a higher standard than those obtained through supplementary acquisition on account of the careful selection process and better breeding. In the years 1934-38 the army administration paid 1,300 to 1,400 Reichsmark for a quality three- to four-year-old horse. As a result of the inflationary economic situation, during the war the price for a horse of the same quality climbed to 1,900 to 2,600 Reichsmark. The state paid as much as 3,000 to 4,000 Reichsmark for race, saddle or tournament horses which were conscripted as part of the supplementary acquisition program.

However, the horse population of the German Reich, which by 1939 had climbed back up to 3,800,000, was insufficient to supply the Wehrmacht with the required numbers of saddle, draft and pack animals. As early as 1936 it was necessary to purchase horses abroad. The source countries were Hungary, Romania, Czechoslovakia and Ireland.

The Wehrmacht was able to acquire 435,000 captured horses, mainly from the armies of Poland, France and the Soviet Union, in the early years of the war. In the further course of the war a total of more than 1,400,000 horses were requisitioned (and paid for)in all the occupied countries and a further 10,000 bought from neutral and friendly nations.

The total number of horses and mules used by the German Armed Forces during the Second World War thus stood at approximately 2,750,000.

The 3rd Remount Committee, Berlin, on the job. The members of this committee were experts of the highest order, their "horse sense" was almost proverbial. Thanks to their abilities the peacetime German army was provided with top-quality horses.

THE CAVALRY SCHOOL AND SPORT RIDING

The buildings of the tradition-rich Hanover Cavalry School proved inadequate to meet the demands of a greatly-expanded Wehrmacht. Consequently, in 1937-38 the training establishment had to be moved to Krampnitz near Potsdam. There it moved into the army's most modern barracks installation, a spacious facility built on the shore of Lake Krampnitz. In the photo, in front of the tower of the Krampnitz school's main guardhouse is the Cavalry Instruction Troop, mounted entirely on chestnut horses, and on the right, on the white horses, the Cavalry Instruction and Testing Battalion's bugler corps.

Any picture of the Wehrmacht cavalry would be incomplete without a brief description of sport riding. The Versailles Treaty did not allow the Reichsheer central training facilities for cavalry. Nevertheless, a cavalry school was set up in Hanover, the site of the old army's Military Riding Institute. In order to avoid difficulties with the states of the Entente the school was given the following title: Horse Breaking Institute for Infantry Officer Riding Horses. In fact, the school turned out first-class riding instructors who, after the First World War, were to ensure a uniform standard of rider training in the forces in keeping with the riding manual. The school's second main purpose was conducting officer candidate training courses for the cavalry.

The regiments sent only their most talented young officers and non-commissioned officers for training as riding instructors, especially since the cavalry school's capacity was restricted on account of the tight financial situation. The instructor corps obviously consisted of officers who were masters of their trade in the saddle. It is no wonder, then, that a riding elite was created in the ten years after the First World War, one which had an affect on the field forces by way of the trained riding instructors. The latter was of special significance to the Reichsheer, whose mobility depended for the most part on well-trained riders, drivers and of course horses. It should be emphasized once again that such motorization as was permitted by the conditions of the Versailles Treaty was used up in seven motor transport battalions, each consisting of a battalion headquarters and three companies, and seven batteries of motorized artillery. By comparison the 100,000-man army had an establishment of 40,234 riding and draft horses plus 991 pack animals, resulting in a ratio of 2.7 men to each horse. These few numbers make it clear that rider and driver training and its testing in peacetime, including in sporting events, was not and end in itself or the cultivation of the expensive passion of a few officers, but instead was an official necessity.

Oberleutnant Pollay, Hanover Cavalry School, on the East Prussian "Kronos," winner in the individual and team dressage events at the 1936 Olympic Games in Berlin.

The cavalry came in for much criticism, not least because it was perceived as an elite. This also applied to the army riding and driving schools, which in the view of many unqualified critics only served to satisfy the sporting ambitions of a few officers. In fact the schools turned out first-class riding and driving instructors who passed on their skills to the army's horse-mounted and horse-drawn units. A large proportion of the training course participants were non-commissioned officers, but they also included qualified enlisted men. Wachtmeister Arlt on "Leopard" at Krampnitz in 1942.

After several Reichswehr officers achieved prominence in the 1920's for their riding feats at home and abroad, in 1928 a team of officers from the cavalry school attracted international attention in the USA. This came at a time when Germany was still cut off from many former enemy nations. In 1930 the cavalry school formed a Department III, dedicated exclusively to training in the various aspects of sport riding. The acquired level of performance now had to be constantly tested in international competitions. In this sense German officer teams took part in nearly every important national and international competitions in the decade from 1930 to 1940. In the beginning, however, the dominant teams internationally were those of the Italian, French and Swedish armies; the Italians were virtually untouchable in the field of show jumping. But then the team from the Hanover Cavalry School succeeded in winning the international competitions for the Coppa d'Oro, a gold cup half a meter tall donated by the Italian dictator Mussolini, in the years 1931, 1932 and 1933. With three victories in a row the trophy passed into the permanent possession of the cavalry school. Apart from countless individual victories, the horsemen in the field-gray uniform won 36 national prizes from 1930 to 1940 alone; however, the German officer-horsemen achieved their greatest success at the 1936 Olympic Games in Berlin. They won all six gold medals as well as one silver. Such dominance in all three disciplines ¨- dressage, jumping and military ¨- was considered impossible by the experts and has never been repeated.

These successes represented more than a mere validation of the method of rider training developed and used by the German Army and its system for training young horses compared to the comparable practices of other armies or states. The Wehrmacht riding manual, H.Dv. 12 of 1937, has remained, in large parts verbatim, the basis of classic rider training in Germany, a fact of which few horsemen are aware today.

In the course of structural changes within the army, in 1937-38 the cavalry school had to be moved from Hanover to Krampnitz, near Potsdam. In addition to the cavalry school, whose sole purpose had become the training of officers and officer candidates, the army established a cavalry instruction and test battalion at Krampnitz. Also created at Krampnitz at the same time was an army riding and driving school, whose primary function was to train riding and driving instructors for all elements of the service. The former Driver Training Detachment remained in Hanover, later becoming the Transportation Troops School.

As high as the standard of training provided by the Army Riding and Driving School was, the school's capacity and that of the thirteen Military Area Riding and Driving Schools was insufficient to supply a million-man army, one which was largely dependent on horses, with carefully-trained riders, drivers and horses. There was a shortage of trained riders and horses as early as 1939-1940, preventing the 1st Cavalry Division, which was then being formed, from reaching planned strengths.

This shortage made itself even more strongly felt in 1943, when a new army cavalry was supposed to be reestablished. One of the chief reasons for this shortfall was the creation in 1938 of the so-called "fast troops," in which all motorized units were combined with horsemen and bicycle troops. Apart from the fact that horsemen and bicyclists were no longer fast in comparison to motor vehicles, they soon became "outdated, poor cousins" in this new arrangement and found themselves in a situation from which they could not free themselves. The situation improved a little after the "fast troops" were disbanded; on April 1, 1943 the horsemen and bicycle troops were transferred to the infantry (In 2). Unfortunately it was too late for meaningful changes. Since the horsemen had for all intents and purposes been mounted infantry since the final years of the Reichswehr, this solution, had it been realized sooner, would have done much to retain the substance of the cavalry and would have contributed to a better situation for all non-motorized troops.

The Coppa d'Oro. This prize, a gold cup, was established by Mussolini. It was the most valuable prize – in an ideal and a material sense – in international sport riding.

The bugler corps of the Cavalry School – Army Riding and Driving School at Krampnitz was mounted entirely on white horses.

Bibliography

1. von Zeska, Major: Das Buch vom Heer, OKW 1940.

2. Zieger, Dr. med. vet. Wilhelm: Das deutsche Heeresveterinärwesen im Zweiten Weltkrieg, 1973.

3. Reibert, W.: Der Dienstunterricht im Heer, Ausgabe für den Reiter, 1938.

4. von Rauchhaupt, Volrad, Oberst Rtd.: Die deutsche Kavallerie zwischen den beiden letzten Kriegen, 1958.

5. Schlicht, Adolf/Angolia, John R.: Die Deutsche Wehrmacht 1933-45, band 1, Das Heer, 1992.

6. Glodkowski, Bruno, Major Rtd.: Deutsche Wehrsprache, in books.

7. Deutsche Reiterhefte, Volumes 1937-1941.

8. von Stein, Hans Rudolf, Major Rtd.: "Feldgrau" Volume 1955: Die deutsche Kavallerie 1939-1945.

9. von Unruh, Generalmajor: Freiwilligen dienen!, 1939.

10. Kern, Erich: General von Pannwitz und seine Kosaken, 1971.

11. Behrens, Wilhelm, Generalleutnant Rtd./Kühn, Dietrich, Rittmeister, Rtd.: Geschichte des Reiter-Regiment 1, Teil I, 1962, and Teil II 1965.

12. Stolz, Gerd/Grieser, Eberhard, Major Rtd.: Geschichte des Kavallerie-Regiment 5, 1975.

13. Jeffke, G.W., Hauptmann Rtd.: Geschichte des Kavallerie- Regiment 8, in books.

14. H.Dv. 11/1 Das Truppenpferd, 1937.
H.Dv. 12   Reitervorschrift, 1937.
H.Dv. 299/2   Die Reiterschwadron, 1937.
H.Dv. 299/3   Die Radfahrerschwadron, 1937
H.Dv.299/6   Die Maschinengewehrschwadron, 1937.
H.Dv. 299/10 Die Aufklärungsabteilungen (mot) u. (tmot), 1939.
H.Dv. 316 Pionierdienst aller Waffen, 1935.
H.Dv. 476/2 Das allgemeine Heeresgerät, 1936
Teil 2 Pferde- und Tragtierausrüstung.

15. National Ministry of Defense, later OKH: Jahrbuch des deutschen Heeres, Volumes 1936-1940.

16. Bayer, Hannes: Kavallerie Divisionen der Waffen-SS, 1982.

17. National War Measures Act, Second Revised Edition, 1944

18. War Correspondents of the Propaganda Companies: Ross und Reiter am Feind, Band 1, various publications.

19. General der Infanterie in the OKH - 1 Cavalry: Überblick über die Entwicklung der deutsche Kavallerie vor und in diesem Krieg, 1945.

20. Tessin, Georg: Verbände und Truppen der deutschen Wehrmacht und Waffen-SS 1939-1945, 1962.

21. Fischer, Karl: Waffen- und schiesstechnischer Leitfaden, 1943; also additional army manuals, various issues of Reibert and other literature concerning the cavalry of the Wehrmacht.

Photo Credits

Regimental Tradition Associations of the:
1st Horse Regiment, 2nd Horse Regiment, 3rd Cavalry Regiment, 5th Cavalry Regiment, 6th Cavalry Regiment, 7th Horse Regiment, 8th Cavalry Regiment, 9th Cavalry Regiment, 13th Cavalry Regiment, 15th Cavalry Regiment, 18th Cavalry Regiment, Cavalry Regiment Center (31st and 32nd Horse Regiments), "ALA" later PzALA.

Other photos were provided by:
Hanns Bayer, Conrad Müller, Hans Schenk, Heinrich Schmidt, Winfried Schott, Heiner Schubert, Hans Otto Wachter.

All other illustrations from the author's collection.

I wish to express my thanks to all those not mentioned by name who contributed to this book by providing photos or helping in other ways.